HORSE FACTS

HORSE FACTS

Susan McBane
&
Helen Douglas-Cooper

FALL RIVER PRESS

This 2009 edition published by Fall River Press,
by arrangement with Quantum Publishing.
6 Blundell Street
London
N7 9BH

Senior Editor Susanna Clarke
Art Editor Anita Ruddell
Designers Hazel Eddington, Frances Austen
Illustrator John Francis
Other Illustrators David Kemp, Sandra Pond, Will Giles
Picture Manager Joanna Wiese
Art Director Nick Buzzard
Publishing Director Janet Slingsby

Fall River Press
122 Fifth Avenue
New York, NY 10011

ISBN: 978-1-4351-1183-7

Printed and bound in Singapore

10 9 8 7 6 5 4 3 2 1

CONTENTS

Section 1
THE NATURE OF THE HORSE
The Origins of the Horse 8 • How Horses Spread 10
The Domestication of the Horse 12 • The Working Horse 14
The Horse in War 16 • The Sporting Horse 18
How Horses Think 20 • How Horses Learn 22
How Horses Sleep 24 • How Horses See 26
How Horses Hear 28 • How Horses Communicate 30
The Points of the Horse 32 • Colors and Markings 34
How the Horse Moves 36 • Coat and Grooming 38
Teeth and Hooves 40 • Breeding 42 • Foalhood 44
Health 46

Section 2
HORSE BREEDS
Breeds and Types 50 • Breeds of the World 54 • Arab 56 • Thoroughbred 58
Quarter-horse 60 • Mustang 62 • Appaloosa 64 • Standardbred 66 • Saddlebred 68
Tennessee Walking Horse 69 • Palomino 70 • Pinto 71 • Pony Of The Americas 72 • Canadian Cutting Horse 73
Falabella 74 • Criollo 75 • Peruvian Paso 76 • Paso Fino 77 • Galiceno 78 • Mangalarga 79 • Exmoor 80 • Dartmoor 81 • Fell 82
Dales 83 • New Forest 84 • Connemara 85 • Shetland 86 • Highland 87 • Welsh Ponies 88 • Cleveland Bay 90 • Hackney 91
Shire 92 • Suffolk Punch 93 • Irish Draught 94 • Irish Half-Bred 95 • Anglo-Arab 96 • French Trotter 97 • Camargue 98
Percheron 100 • Draught Breton 101 • Friesian 102 • Belgian Heavy Draft 103 • Franches Montagnes 104 • Trakehner 105
Hanoverian 106 • Oldenburg 108 • East Friesian 109 • Holstein 110 • Schleswig Heavy Draft 111 • Lipizzaner 112 • Haflinger 114
Gelderland 115 • Swedish Warm-Blood 116 • Swedish Ardennes 117 • Fredericksborg 118 • Knabstrup 119 • Døle 120
Fjord 121 • Finnish 122 • Icelandic 123 • Salerno 124 • Italian Heavy Draft 125 • Andalusian 126 • Altér Real 128 • Lusitano 129
Skyros 130 • Bosnian 131 • Tarpan 132 • Konik 133 • Wielkopolski 134 • Kladruber 135 • Shagya Arab 136 • Furioso 137
Murakosi 138 • Orlov Trotter 139 • Don 140 • Budyonny 141 • Akhal Teké 142 • Tersky 143 • Karabakh 144
Vladimir Heavy Draft 145 • Barb 146 • Caspian 147 • Persian Arab 148 • Basuto 149
Manipur 150 • Mongolian Wild Horse 151 • Burma 152 • Java 153 • Sumba 154
Australian Stock Horse 155 • Australian Pony 156 • Brumby 157

Index 158
Credits 160

THE
NATURE
OF THE
HORSE

The Origins of the Horse

The earliest horse ancestor, known as Hyracotherium (formerly as Eohippus), was discovered in North America from fossils about 50 million years old, and similar fossils have been found in Europe. It was a lamb-sized mammal with four toes on its front feet and three on its hind feet.

Strains of Hyracotherium existed from 50 to 38 million years ago. It was a forest and swamp-dwelling animal; grassy plains not yet having developed. It appeared first in North America, and migrated from there across the landmass into Europe (the two were not at that time separated by the Atlantic Ocean).

As the Earth's climate changed, so did the vegetation. Parts of the Earth became cooler and drier and grasses and open plains evolved; as this happened the early horse types became longer-legged and faster, and the number of toes was reduced to three all round. Two groups of three-toed horses emerged: browsers, who fed on leaves; and grazers, who fed on grasses. Browsers appeared first, but became extinct about 11 million years ago. Grazers, which appeared about 10 to 15 million years ago, were larger and longer-legged than browsers and were more efficient feeders. Some historians claim that Alexander the Great's charger, Bucephalus, had three toes on each leg, with only the central one bearing weight, and that it was thus a throwback to a primeval form of horse.

Above: The Exmoor Pony is thought to have existed in south-western England since prehistoric times. It is believed to be descended from the original Celtic pony of western Europe. The breed has remained very pure, and is thought to have changed little since primitive times.

Below: Eohippus (left), also known as Hyracotherium, is one of the earliest equine ancestors. It lived around 50 million years ago. Dinohippus (center), a descendant of Eohippus, first appeared about 15 million years ago. Early Equus (right) evolved from Dinohippus.

Gradually, one-toed horse types developed from among the grazing types. They had larger bodies, longer legs, and enlarged jaws and skulls, and were thus much better adapted to grazing and running. Like Hyracotherium, the one-toed horse types seem to have originated in North and Central America, with one group known to have migrated to South America. Horse types also migrated across the still-existing Bering land bridge between Alaska and what is now Russia, but once this sank below the sea, European, African and Asian horse types were cut off from those in the Americas.

The one-toed horse type is known as Equus, and is the forerunner of the modern horse and its relatives such as the donkey and the zebra.

There were many different species of Equus, but most had become extinct by the end of the last Ice Age, including all those in North America. The types that survived in Europe and Asia diversified into larger and smaller types.

Above right: This family tree shows how, over the course of about 55 million years, a diverse range of horselike animals evolved from the four-toed Hyracotherium (Eohippus). Many branches of the horse family died out, leaving one main group of one-toed horses from which Equus, the modern horse, evolved.

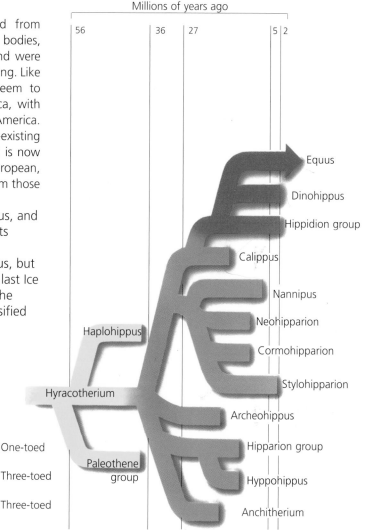

Millions of years ago

56   36   27   5 2

Equus

Dinohippus

Hippidion group

Calippus

Nannipus

Neohipparion

Haplohippus

Cormohipparion

Stylohipparion

Hyracotherium

Archeohippus

Hipparion group

Paleothene group

Hyppohippus

Anchitherium

One-toed

Three-toed

Three-toed

Below right: The zebra is one of the horse's closest relatives, also being descended from Equus. It displays many features of primitive pony types, such as the upright mane and stocky body. Zebra markings sometimes appear on the flanks and legs of ancient breeds such as the Tarpan and the Mongolian Wild Horse.

How Horses Spread

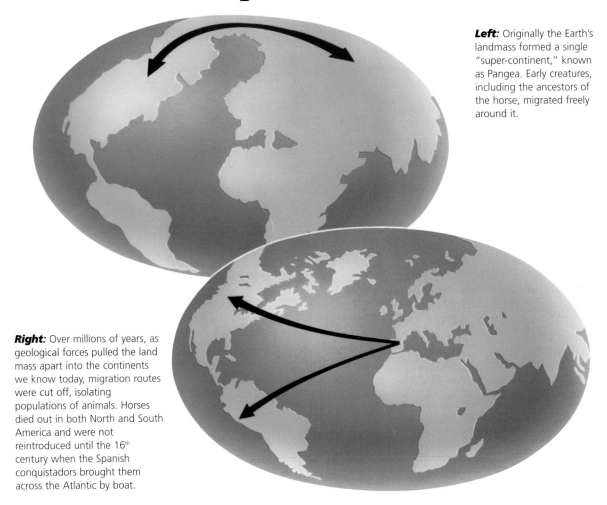

Left: Originally the Earth's landmass formed a single "super-continent," known as Pangea. Early creatures, including the ancestors of the horse, migrated freely around it.

Right: Over millions of years, as geological forces pulled the land mass apart into the continents we know today, migration routes were cut off, isolating populations of animals. Horses died out in both North and South America and were not reintroduced until the 16th century when the Spanish conquistadors brought them across the Atlantic by boat.

Information on the early horse types is very incomplete, but it seems that they first spread from their evolutionary homeland in North America over landmasses very different from today's continents. As the landmasses split up at the end of the last Ice Age, horse groups developed simultaneously in different areas. However, because Australia split from the main landmass many millions of years before horse types migrated that far, no horses existed there until they were introduced by the early settlers during the 18th century. No early horse fossils have been found in Australia.

It is now thought that there were a number of different types of Equus in Europe and Asia, some being pony types, others more like small horses, and that they developed according to the environment in which they lived—those living in wild, wet areas remaining small; others in areas with good grazing growing larger.

It is also thought that these types became quite widely dispersed, and crossbred, even before man intervened in the development of the horse.

Ever since man first domesticated the horse, in the Middle and Far East around 3000 BC, he has been instrumental in distributing the different horse types around the world.

The nomadic tribes of central Asia, who were probably the first people to domesticate the horse, would have taken their horses with them as they wandered across quite large areas of the continent. Conquering tribes took horses with them to pull their chariots, and to use as pack animals.

When the Celts were driven into western Europe, and eventually to Britain, they took their Tarpan type horses (see page 132) and crossed them with indigenous horses to produce the Celtic pony, which they used to pull their chariots. In Britain, the Celtic pony provided the basis of many of the modern native breeds.

The Romans brought many different types of horses to Britain, including Friesian horses from northern Europe, from which the Dales and Fell ponies developed.

When the Moors invaded Europe, beginning in the eighth century, they brought with them many thousands of horses of Arab breeding, from which the Andalusian and many other European breeds were created.

In the 16th century the Spanish conquistadors invaded America, taking with them a variety of ornately caparisoned Iberian, and thereby reintroducing the horse into North America.

The horse had returned home.

Above: The Mongolian pony is descended from the ancient native ponies of Mongolia, which the local tribes used as pack animals. These nomadic people traveled widely.

Below: At the Lascaux caves in southern France there are drawings of prehistoric horses that appear to resemble both the Mongolian Wild Horse of north-east Asia and the Exmoor pony.

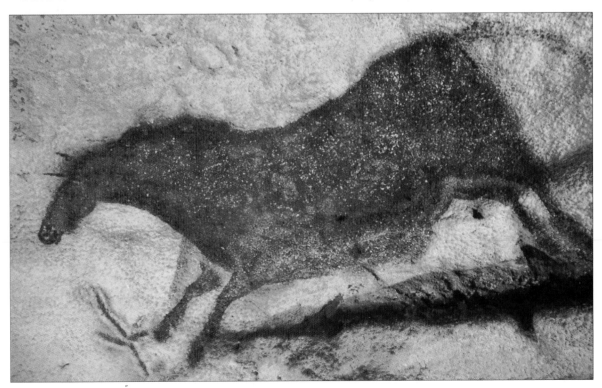

The Domestication of the Horse

The horse was domesticated in the Far East by early civilizations about 5,000 years ago (around 3,000 BC). Some experts believe this took place in Asiatic Russia and others that this happened in the ancient Fertile Crescent comprising Assyria and Babylonia. However, Stone Age drawings on rocks and in caves have shown what appears to be a head-collar of some kind, so it is possible that more primitive peoples had some kind of control over early horses.

Initially, primitive tribes would have followed herds of wild horses, hunting them for meat. Domestication probably first occurred when young animals were captured and kept tethered or in pens. These animals were used for meat and milk, and would gradually have become accustomed to human attention. Mares in season would have been tethered on the outskirts of a tribe's territory, so that wild stallions could come and mate with them.

These nomadic horse-owners soon realized that a horse could be made to carry goods and equipment, and so the horse began to be used as a pack animal. It has been suggested by historian Anthony Dent that the first riders were the pregnant wives of tribal leaders, who were put on horses to enable them to keep up with the tribe's nomadic wanderings.

The earliest widespread use of domesticated horses was as pack and harness animals. It is likely that even at this early stage in the history of the horse's domestication, the horse types diverged into harness types and riding types in different parts of the world, and that people traded in these different horses so that they had the kind they needed.

Man began to ride horses quite early on, but in war early civilizations such as the Egyptians and Greeks used horses mainly to pull their chariots. The Persians, however, were excellent horsemen, and by 500 BC, had a powerful cavalry with horses able to carry heavy armor and weapons. The ancient Greeks were also good horsemen, but the Romans, who had mounted cavalry, were not especially so.

Below: A piece from the west side of the Parthenon Frieze (477–432 BC), showing two horsemen at the canter taking part in a procession. Although bridles and bits had been invented at this stage, saddles had not. The Greeks were good horsemen, and took great interest in the best methods of training and riding horses.

Right: A Greek seal inscribed with the name of Darius I, who reigned from 548 to 486 BC. It depicts a king hunting from a horse-drawn chariot. Horses were used for drawing chariots long before they were ridden.

Below: An ancient Persian relief showing a battle between two mounted warriors. The ancient Persians were the first to use the horse for riding. They were excellent horsemen, and developed a very efficient cavalry.

The Working Horse

Since it was first domesticated, the horse has been used for all types of work. Even today, every horse is, in practice, working for its living, whether it is a child's pony, a racehorse, or a farm horse.

In the beginning, the horse's main role was as a pack animal, and it continued to be used in this role up until the early part of the 20th century. To start with, the smaller, lighter types were used for this kind of work while the larger, more powerful animals were used as war horses. However, with the invention of firearms, armor was abandoned and a different type of horse was needed in battle, freeing the heavier horses for other types of work.

With the advent of industrialization, heavy loads of equipment and goods needed to be moved across the country, and the very large, heavy draft breeds such as the Shire and the Clydesdale were developed. During the 19th century, horses were also used for towing barges along canals, and for moving coal and equipment around the coalmines.

Horses have also played an important part in agriculture. In the beginning, plows were pulled by oxen, being too heavy for the lighter breeds of working horses. However, by the 18th century mechanized farm equipment was beginning to be used. Speed and intelligence were needed in the animals being used to pull it, and draft horses came into their own for agricultural work.

Horses were also the main means of transport for people. As better roads began to be built in the 19th

century, and the art of carriage-making reached its highest standards, coaches became lighter and faster, and very elegant horses, such as Trotters and Hackneys, were in demand to pull them.

With the arrival first of the railways and then the motor car, the horse was no longer needed for transport or agricultural work and it looked as if many of the draft breeds might die out. However, businesses are now realizing that, for short trips, horses are more economical for deliveries than motorized vans, and are beginning to use them.

Above: Horsedrawn buses were once a common sight. Animals used for public transportation, unlike the carriage-horses of the wealthy, often led a hard life, working on slippery cobbled streets.

Left: Heavy draft breeds like the Shire were often associated with agricultural work such as plowing. However, the very large draft breeds did not come into their own for this type of work until the end of the 18th century, when the invention of more sophisticated farm machinery required the use of horses that combined great physical strength with intelligence.

THE POLICE HORSE

It is in police work—for example, in the Royal Canadian Mounted Police (above)—that the horse/man relationship reaches one of its most refined levels. Police horses are trained to overcome almost completely their natural flight-or-fight instinct, and to face up to situations like violent crowds, gunfire, and physical force from rioters. They must go wherever their rider asks, at any hour of the day or night, alone or in company, without question.

In their initial training, they are taught to approach a potentially frightening object or situation and are turned away from it, with great praise, just before the trainer feels the horse might object. In this way, the horse never develops resistance to its work, and comes to trust its rider implicitly.

Above: Although horses are no longer needed in most countries for farming and transportation work, several of the draft breeds from the heyday of the working horse, such as these Percherons, have survived, and are valued for their own sakes. They are used for demonstrations and showing, and, in a small way, for work.

Right: Ranching in Texas, where the horse is still used in one of its traditional working roles, for herding cattle. The Quarter-horse, first bred in the eastern United States, was found to have a particular talent for this type of work. It was bred in large numbers and became the favorite horse of the cowboy.

The Horse in War

Above: A section of the Bayeux Tapestry showing the Norman cavalry in action at the Battle of Hastings in 1066. By this time the Normans had developed a highly skilled cavalry, and the English footsoldiers were no match for it.

It is truly said that empires have been built on the horse's back. Without the strength, speed, and willingness of the horse to do man's bidding, all-conquering civilizations from the earliest days of the horse's domestication right up to the 20th century could not have conquered other peoples and spread their cultures throughout the world.

In the early days horses were used in battle mainly to pull chariots, but gradually the use of cavalry developed. The Persians, who were expanding their empire around 500 BC, used cavalry to great effect.

Much of the success of the Islamic empire as it spread across most of Europe was due to its fast and highly disciplined cavalry. The European warhorse of this time, in contrast, was heavy and slow, as it had to carry up to 500 lb (225 kg) of arms and protective armor, as well as its rider, into battle.

With the invention of firearms, heavy armor became obsolete, and new types of cavalry developed. These fell into three groups. The dragoons were mounted on heavy, cob types; the lancers were mounted on lighter horses, and were used for sudden assaults and fast flanking movements; and the Hussars, also used for sudden attacks, were mounted on light, fast horses.

During the 19th century, with the development of shrapnel and automatic weapons, the value of the cavalry charge gradually declined, although horses were still used for artillery and troop movements, and very large numbers of horses were used in all campaigns until after World War I.

HORSE ARMOR

In the Middle Ages, armor reached its zenith as horse and rider were clad in more and more concealing plates of intricately jointed metal, which, of course, became increasingly heavy. Knights often had to be hoisted onto their horses. Horses' face-plates often had spikes on the forehead, giving the horse the appearance of a metal unicorn. The body armor covered the whole horse down to its elbows and stifles, protruding at the front to allow for foreleg and knee movement. Neck armor was also made from jointed plates of metal to allow for movement. Horse armor continued to be used until the end of the 16th century, by which time the increasing use of firearms and cannon had rendered it obsolete. The illustration shows early 16th-century Spanish armor.

In World War I, well-loved family horses, children's ponies and commercial horses were commandeered into the army by force, never to be returned to their families or owners. To put down a horse rather than allow it to be taken was regarded as treason. In modern times horses are used by armies all over the world for ceremonial purposes.

Above: The Charge of the Light Brigade in 1854 was one of the most disastrous cavalry charges ever. Out of 673 horses that charged the Russian artillery, only 260 survived. The development of automatic weapons and shrapnel during the 19th century gradually made massed cavalry charges of this sort obsolete.

Left: During World War I millions of horses were used on all parts of the front, and losses were appalling. The Royal Scots Greys arrived at the Belgian frontier soon after the outbreak of war, and the famous gray horses had to be stained chestnut in order to camouflage them, and prevent the enemy identifying their formation.

The Sporting Horse

Equestrian sports go from strength to strength, and are increasingly popular with both riders and spectators. One of the oldest surviving horseback sports is hunting. In the beginning, the stag was the main quarry, but now, in English-speaking countries, it is the fox. In both the USA and Australia, hunting is based on the British model.

Polo is another ancient sport, and is thought to have originated in Persia about 2,000 years ago. From there it spread to China, Mongolia, Japan, and eventually India, where it was discovered by the British in the 19th century. Its popularity has since spread all over the world. It makes exacting demands on the horses, requiring considerable speed, agility, stamina, and courage.

Horseracing has been popular around the world for many centuries, but since the early 18th century it has developed into a major sporting industry.

Another sport that is increasing in popularity is driving, and many breeds of horse that were originally used as carriage-horses have found a new role in this sport. Combined driving, which was introduced in 1969, is the equivalent of a three-day event, and includes a dressage test, a cross-country marathon, and an obstacle-course in the showring.

Horse shows that included both competitive events and showing classes began to be held in the late 19th century. These came to include showjumping and dressage events as well as the show classes in which horses are judged on type and conformation (make and shape). The latter are more leisurely but can be just as exciting to their enthusiasts, and even tiny children can compete in lead-line classes, which sets many off on the road to becoming a champion.

The breeding of horses for competition rather than military use has resulted in finer, faster horses, even in carriage-driving, and has improved many breeds, or at least changed them beyond all recognition. This particularly applies to the many European

Above: The ancient Chinese, Tartars, Mongols, and Greeks all raced their horses. In modern times, racing as a sport took off with the development of the Thoroughbred, which is still the fastest breed of horse in the world.

Above: Polo is one of the roughest, toughest games played today, and playing in the snow adds an extra dimension of excitement. Polo ponies must be brave and obedient; they must be able to stop and turn like lightning.

Left: The Master and Huntsman of a French hunt. Hunting is one of the oldest sports. In the past many different animals were hunted, but for the last two centuries the fox has been the most popular quarry in most countries.

THE OLYMPIC SPORTS

The three modern Olympic equestrian sports are showjumping, dressage, and eventing.

Showjumping

The origins of showjumping lie in hunting. At the Dublin Show in 1868, a "high leap" and a "wide leap" were first used to test horses for the hunting field. In 1881, a permanent jumping course was built there and showjumping began to develop as a sport in its own right. In France in 1900, jumping competitions were held with the Olympic Games.

Dressage

Dressage developed from the high-school equitation of the 15th to 18th centuries which was popular in the royal courts of Europe. Movements that had originally been developed for use in battle were combined into a demonstration of horsemanship that showed off the stamina, agility, and obedience of the horse and the skills of the rider.

Eventing

The origins of eventing lie in the battlefield, as it developed out of the endurance rides that were used to test cavalry horses. At the beginning of the 20th century, the first three-day event was held, in France. It began with a dressage test, followed by a gruelling cross-country endurance ride, and concluded with a showjumping test (added partly to increase public interest in eventing). At this time three-day events were purely military affairs, and it was not until after World War II that civilians could compete. Eventing was first included in the Olympics in 1912, and is the ultimate all-round test of a horse.

Showjumping

Dressage

warm-blood breeds such as the Hanoverian, the Holstein, and the Trakehner, which now have a great deal of Thoroughbred blood in them to provide the speed, quality, and quick reactions needed in today's sports horse.

Many forms of equine competition involve large sums of money, both paid for and won by horses, as well as sponsorship deals, but the main attraction for the public lies in watching the superb achievements and performances of racehorses, showjumpers, eventers, carriage-horses, trotters and pacers.

Eventing

How Horses Think

Horses certainly do think—to survive in the wild over millions of years they have had to develop the ability to think extremely quickly (although their initial "startle" reflex on becoming aware of dangers such as a predator is more instinct than thinking). Once they have become aware of a potential danger, they must quickly assess the situation, and decide whether or not to run away, or just move to keep the danger outside their personal space.

Some horses seem to show more intelligent thought than others. For example, some work out quite quickly how to undo their stable bolts and escape—a few even learn how to undo the doors of other horses in the barn and let them out. This requires both planning and understanding of the outcome of their action.

The ability to look ahead shows high-level thinking ability, and although horses may not be able to plan and look ahead to the extent that humans can, they understand time and know that certain things will happen at a certain time of day; for example feed times. If a horse is thirsty, it has to think to go to the water source. If it is in a field at feed time, it shows thinking ability by wandering over to the gate and looking expectantly (looking ahead) in the direction from which you will come with its feed bucket.

In order, for example, to complete a round of jumps, the horse has to concentrate quite hard, thinking about the various aids its rider is giving it and what

they mean—more impulsion, slow down, turn here—and it has to realize that the jump its rider has aimed it at is the one it is required to clear. It then has to gauge its own strides, or perhaps regulate them in accordance with its rider's instructions, and take off into the air in the right place. Only the horse itself can decide, by thinking quickly, just how high to propel itself into the air. This takes considerable judgment, even with experience and practice, and cannot be done without clear thought.

REASONING POWER

It is often said that horses have no reasoning power; reasoning being the ability to think out a problem or situation and overcome it. Many experienced and sensitive horsemen deny this, knowing from their own experience that horses can solve problems. In one informal experiment, horses were given feeds in buckets with loose lids which they had to remove before they could eat. Most of the horses clearly considered the situation and by various means removed the lids calmly. Only a few bashed frustratedly at the buckets, showing no ability to think through the problem.

In another incident, a mare was caught by one hind leg in a loose wire fence. She was seen to turn her head and look for several seconds at the loop of wire round her leg. She then raised her other hind leg, felt the wire carefully with her (shod) hoof, stepped on the loop pressing it down to the ground, and freed her trapped leg. This is an obvious example of clear thought and reasoning power.

Below left: Mares and foals in domesticity are usually weaned earlier than would happen in the wild. If they are reunited, they will recognize each other.

Below right: Horses that work with cattle have to be very quick-thinking to anticipate the direction the steer or calf will take, and to react instantly.

REACTING TO A THREAT

A horse confronted by something frightening or potentially dangerous will analyze the threat and respond according to the perceived seriousness of the danger. Initially it will show the "startle response"—it will raise its head, prick up its ears, and point them forward, flare its nostrils to take in potentially informative smells, and open its eyes wide to see as much as possible. Its body will be tense and its hind legs will come slightly more forward under the body ready to take its weight if the danger is such that it decides to wheel around and gallop off to safety.

If in the case, for example, of an intruder, the horse decides to stand its ground, it will probably thrust its head forward aggressively, with ears back, nostrils wrinkled up and back and maybe bare its teeth and open the mouth as a warning of its intention to bite if the threatening intruder does not retreat. Should the intruder not retreat, it will threaten more aggressively, moving forward with the expression described, maybe with head low and neck stretched out, lunging out at the intruder with its teeth.

If, in the case of a horse intruder, the other horse does not withdraw, a fight may ensue. Both horses will maintain an angry, aggressive expression and they will bite at each other anywhere within reach. Males in particular often rear up with flailing forelegs, trying to come down on to the back of their opponent and get them down onto the ground where they can be trampled and kicked. They also back into each other, kicking out rapidly in succession with both hind feet. Such kicking is a more common method of fighting for mares.

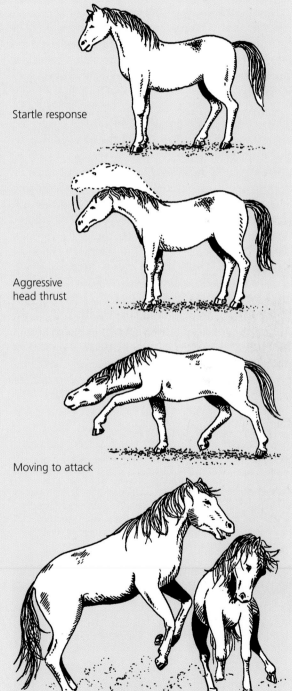

Startle response

Aggressive
head thrust

Moving to attack

Fighting

How Horses Learn

Survival in the wild is often dependent on an ability to adapt rapidly to new conditions. Horses can learn fast if the right training is given.

Horses learn mainly by means of association of ideas. It has been scientifically and practically proven that if a horse can be made to associate a particular task, even an unpleasant or frightening one, with something pleasant, he will tolerate it much more readily. For instance, a horse that does not like being shod will accept it in time if it learns that it will be fed some favourite tidbits, or have a net of sweet hay to nibble at, during the process. If you are trying to teach a horse to move over in the stable, for example by pushing it so that it moves away, and at the same time saying "over," it soon learns to associate the push with the action and before long will move over to a slight pressure on its side or just the word "over." The position of the handler's body is important too. For example, if you stand directly in front of or behind it when saying "over," it will not know which way to move.

Horses learn their daily routine quickly and watch the goings on, listen to the various sounds, and absorb daily happenings. They quickly associate the rattle of feed buckets with the appearance of feed, for instance, and the sight of someone carrying their saddle and bridle with work or going for a hack.

They are also quick to absorb atmosphere and can differentiate between a pleased, praising, or calming tone in the human voice and a sharp, cross, reprimanding tone, or an urging, encouraging one.

Below: At the beginning of its training, the horse learns basic commands like "walk on" and "whoa" on the lunge. Being led by a helper, the horse is shown what the different sounds mean. Soon it learns the commands well enough to work mainly from the voice alone.

KEEP IT SIMPLE

Horses learn short, simple sounds best. Although a stream of words said in a particular tone can convey your feelings—such as calming down or urging on—when you want the horse to perform a particular movement it is best to use short sounds of up to three syllables.

Below: Racehorses are introduced to starting stalls as youngsters by being walked through them, then standing in them; they soon learn that the gates flying open means "gallop."

CIRCUS HORSE

Circus horses, particularly those touring the same route every year, often have to learn new acts regularly, as their audiences will want to see something different each time. However, they never forget their old routines, and can usually be put through a movement after several years' break and perform it faultlessly. Even just the sound of a particular tune can set them off on an old routine.

Left: To reach the high standards required at the Spanish Riding School, horses must learn movements that are progressively more difficult, both mentally and physically; they must show increasing understanding of their riders' requirements, and respond to finer and finer aids.

As horses recognize the actual sound, the tone and inflection of the voice is very important. Always give commands in the same way so as not to confuse the horse. When you buy a new horse, ask the previous owner to demonstrate the exact way in which he or she gave it commands so you can imitate them, even down to their accent if necessary. If the previous owner asked the horse to "trot on" and you use the long drawn-out command "terr-ot," you cannot blame the horse for not complying.

REWARD VERSUS PUNISHMENT

Horses are easily upset and startled, so it is best to use reward training rather than punishment training. For instance, when a horse does something right, praise it consistently by always using the words "good boy" said in the same tone. If it does something wrong, however, it's best to give no response at all but make your aids clearer, then praise it when it does get it right. Most horses do want to please.

There are times when a horse may be blatantly naughty or dominating. In such cases, one sharp smack or crack of the whip used at the same time as saying the word "no" crossly, delivered the instant it does wrong, will convey the message that this behavior is not wanted.

It is essential that both praise and punishment are administered within one second of the horse's action, otherwise the horse cannot connect your response with whatever it did and will learn nothing. It must associate your action with its own, good or bad, in order to learn whether you are pleased or not. This is the way its brain works and is essential to the learning process.

INADVERTENT LEARNING

If a horse comes to associate an action with something unpleasant, it will not want to do it. For example, if a horse receives a painful jab in the mouth every time it jumps, it will quickly learn that jumping means pain and will start refusing; if it is kicked on the hip every time it is mounted it will soon start to become difficult to mount, having learned that the process is unpleasant.

How Horses Sleep

Horses need sleep just as much as humans do, but they don't need the same amount. They need about four hours sleep out of every 24, and take it in roughly half-hour snatches rather than all in one go. The reason for this is, again, their prey/predator lifestyle, which so frequently spills over into domesticity. As creatures of wide open spaces, often with little natural protection such as a lair or den, the horse needs to be constantly on the alert for danger. If it were to spend several hours at a stretch deeply asleep, it would be easy prey for a hunting animal, so it has evolved to sleep for short periods.

The horse does not always sleep at night, but takes some of its sleep during daylight, if allowed to. Many horses that have had morning exercise like to lie down for a nap after their midday feed, imitating the sleep pattern they would adopt in the wild. This can also be seen in horses turned out in fields, who often lie down during the day.

Apart from dozing, there are two kinds of sleep, SWS (shortwave sleep) and REM (rapid eye movement) sleep. Experiments using electrodes to detect electrical brainwaves have shown that in shallow sleep the brainwaves are of a short frequency (SWS): the brain is quite inactive but the sleep is fairly shallow and the horse can be easily awakened.

Deep sleep is experienced when the brain waves are longer. The brain is active during this type of sleep, but the body goes almost into a torpor, making the horse easy to approach but difficult to wake up. During this sleep, the eyes move rapidly from side to side beneath the eyelids, which is why it is called rapid eye movement (REM) sleep. Because the body seems to lose muscle tone during REM sleep, the horse has to lie completely relaxed and flat out on its side in order to experience it, whereas in SWS it can sleep propped on its breastbone. It is likely that horses, like humans, dream during REM sleep.

Lying flat out is obviously dangerous in the wild as it takes a horse several vital seconds to get to its feet and gallop off. It is much safer for the horse to lie propped up as it can get up much more quickly.

From a management point of view, it is essential to give a horse a large enough stable to allow it to lie flat out and experience the deep, refreshing, and essential REM sleep, and to give it a dry, clean, soft bed so it won't be reluctant to lie down and rest. The horse must have enough room that it does not become cast, which happens when it rolls over and becomes trapped on its back because its legs strike the wall of the stall. Horses always pick a smooth, dry spot to sleep when they have a choice: those kept on wet land in winter may be reluctant to lie down often enough, particularly flat out, and may deprive themselves of sleep as a result. Such horses should have access to a well bedded-down, roomy, run-in barn or large shelter.

CAN HORSES SLEEP STANDING UP?

Yes, they can and do. Again, this is a safety feature from the wild. If they are already on their feet (in which position they can either doze or experience SWS) they can be off at a gallop within a couple of seconds of being alerted, usually by other horses or by a sound.

There is a special arrangement of "locking" joints and ligaments in their elbows and stifles (another safety feature) which props the horse on its forelegs keeping it upright. It can rest one hind leg (joints bent, hip down) during this process and still not fall over, but not a foreleg. When alerted, up comes its head throwing the weight on to its hindquarters, which gather underneath it ready to propel it forward out of danger.

Left: In this position a horse will doze, and can also experience shortwave sleep, a shallow kind of sleep. To be able to sleep standing up was a great advantage to the horse in the wild, because it could be off at a gallop within seconds.

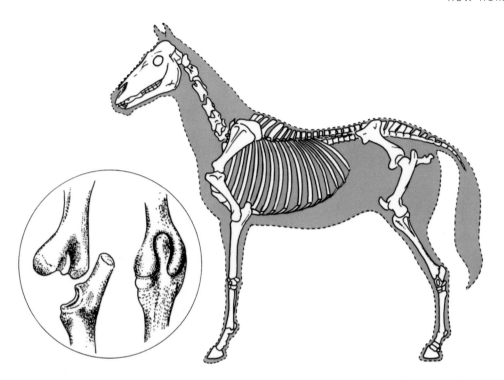

Above: Horses have a special arrangement of "locking" joints and ligaments in their elbows and stifles. When the horse sleeps standing up, these joints lock, propping up the horse on its forehand. It can even relax one hind leg and still not fall over.

Below: Horses need to lie flat out in order to experience REM (rapid eye movement), or deep, sleep. Horses whose stalls are too small, or who feel that they don't have room to lie out like this may deprive themselves of this type of sleep, and become over-tired, short-tempered, or even neurotic as a result.

How Horses See

The horse's eyes are ideal for its existence as a plains-dwelling, grass-eating prey animal, and are similar to those of other prey animals, for example cattle and antelope. Such animals need the widest possible field of vision so that they can see potential predators approaching more or less from all directions. Their eyes are set on the sides of the head, rather than at the front like predators such as cats, dogs, and humans. In their natural state, grass-eaters spend a good 16 hours a day with their heads down, grazing. This position gives them the ability to see all around with a small turn of the head while still eating, without moving the body as humans need to do if they want to see clearly behind them. The only obstruction to the horse's vision in this position is its four thin legs, so it is ideally equipped for most of the time to spot danger. This is the main reason for its good survival rate in the wild, and explains why it is not easy to approach horses in a field without being noticed.

The accompanying diagram shows the horse's actual field of vision when it is looking straight ahead. Its vision is mainly "monocular" (single-eyed), that is, it mostly sees its surroundings as two pictures, one from each eye. This indicates that it is probably capable of thinking about two things at once, at the same time as grazing. It has "binocular" (two-eyed) vision directly in front of it for judging clearly how far away an object is, and to enable it to assess accurately the route in front of it when moving.

For many years the horse was described as having a "ramped retina," because its retina (the screen at the back of the eye on which rays of light carrying images focused) was thought to be sloped. This would require the horse to move its head to bring the images into focus. It is now known that the central part of the retina gives the clearest picture, and this is the reason for the horse's various head movements when trying to see something. It moves its head to direct the rays through the eye lens (which is not as flexible as in human beings) to direct them on to the center of the retina.

The most significant point to emerge is that in order for the horse to have clear vision and, therefore, peace of mind and security, it must have reasonable freedom to move its head and neck as it wishes. If the rider restricts its head unduly, by means of either reins, or equipment such as martingales which "strap down" the head, they are partially blinding the horse. This is one reason why a horse not only goes unwillingly, but

Below: The horse's field of vision enables it to see almost all around it. This gives it the advantage that while it is grazing, it only has to turn its head slightly in order to check that there is no danger approaching from any direction. It is almost impossible to approach unnoticed.

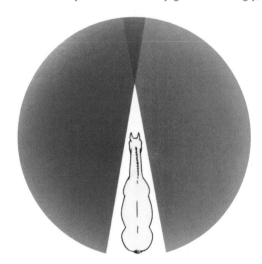

Above: The horse's eyes are set on the sides of its head, and it sees two different pictures, one with each eye. This gives it a very wide field of vision. The small V-shaped area directly in front of its head is the only area where it can see with both eyes and therefore clearly judge distances

Right: The harness of draught horses usually incorporates blinkers to prevent the horse from becoming alarmed by the traffic and other distracting sights that usually surround it in busy street. The blinkers of these Shire horses belonging to a British brewery keep their attention focused on the road ahead.

may fight for its head. The other reason is that a horse naturally panics if over-restricted. Freedom of its head and neck is particularly important when a horse is moving fast or jumping, as it must have clear vision to judge the ground, and the size of obstacles.

To see clearly close in front of it, the horse must arch its neck and draw in its muzzle into a "collected"

position. This directs the rays of light through the top part of the pupil on to the center of the retina. If you watch your horse, you'll see it do this to look at you or something you are carrying when close to it, or to inspect some close-up object or the ground in front of it.

The horse's pupil is a horizontal oval rather than a circle, giving it a wide but rather shallow panoramic field of vision, and it can be easily startled by things not quite in view above its head. Young horses backed for the first time are often frightened by a rider sitting up above them. It's advisable for the rider to crouch low over the withers at first, gradually assuming a more upright position.

The inability to perceive depth, except when looking immediately in front of it, accounts for the fact that the horse will shy sideways away from something which startles it because it cannot tell what it is. It will, if permitted, turn and face the object head on, from a safe distance, look at it with both eyes and satisfy its curiosity.

GLORIOUS TECHNICOLOR

Horse spectrum

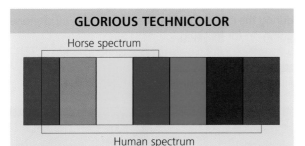

Human spectrum

An old belief of some horsemen was that horses are color blind. Research shows, however, that they do have similar color-discerning cells in their eyes to humans. They can, it seems, see yellow best, and orange and red. They can distinguish green quite well but have difficulty with blue and violet. It is important to school your horse over different colored jumps and use all the colors of the spectrum to accustom it to anything it might meet in the jumping arena.

IT'S KEEPING ITS EYE ON YOU

When you are riding, your horse can see your legs, whether or not you are carrying a whip, and when you move it to use it (which is why it may often anticipate your whip aid and move before you apply it). When you are riding a bend or a circle, its inside eye can make visual contact with yours, if you position the horse correctly, and you can just about look each other in the eye.

How Horses Hear

Horses are very sensitive to sound, and can hear high- and low-pitched noises that humans are unable to pick up.

The pinna, or funnel part of the ear, picks up the soundwaves and directs them down inside the head where a network of bones and chambers, together with the eardrum, transmit and amplify them for special nerves to pick up. These nerves in turn transmit these messages to the brain, which translates the sounds into meaning if they are familiar, or alerts the horse to something strange in its environment if they are not.

A horse does not automatically panic at an unfamiliar sound; it will pay attention to it and remember it. If something happens at the same time as the sound, it will, in future, associate the happening with that sound, and this is an important part of training and learning.

Horses' hearing is sharper than that of humans; they can hear things like other horses calling, car engines (which they can tell apart from each other), and doors opening, before a person can pick them up and from much farther away. Horses that are boarded out, for example, soon come to recognize their owners' car engines and associate the noise with the appearance of that particular person. They will often pick up the sound and long before the staff in the stable.

Horses are extremely sensitive to the nature of a sound and its volume. There is never any need to shout at a horse unless it is a very dominant animal, either attacking or really pushing its weight around, in which case volume can help get the better of it. Tone of voice is usually more effective than volume; a cross growl when the horse is doing wrong, and an up-and-down, pleased tone for praise.

Screaming and screeching often frighten horses, whereas soft monotones calm them down.

However, some sounds that might be thought to frighten them, such as blasting in a quarry or police sirens, do not always do so.

Horses are as agitated by constant, raucous sound as humans are. In racing stables for instance, the best trainers insist on a quiet period during the afternoon after morning work, grooming, and the midday feed, so that the horses can lie down and rest or have a sleep.

Some horses prefer a busy atmosphere where they can see and hear what is going on around them, and others like peace and quiet. It is important to watch your horse and try to tell by its behavior and expression which category it falls into. If it seems slightly (or very) tense, its ears flicking around a lot, not resting much during the day, it could be that there is too much noise going on for its liking.

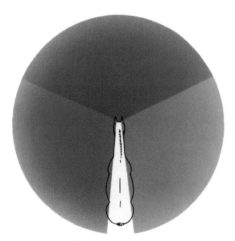

Above: The position of the horse's ears on the sides of its head enables it to hear almost all around it. Each ear can pick up sounds to the front and side, leaving a gap immediately behind it which it can cover with a small turn of its head.

Below: The mare has one ear back and one forward, indicating that she is listening to what is going on all around.

Above: The horse on the right is interested in what is going on around it, while its companion is showing signs of annoyance.

MUSIC

Experiments carried out with mares at the Irish National Stud some years ago showed that horses like music, but are selective in their tastes. Most horses like calming or cheerful instrumental music and are agitated by heavy, loud unmelodious music such as rock. Vocal music is also not as welcome to them as instrumental music.

Dressage performed to music is now popular in many countries and the horses really seem to enjoy it. They appear perky, majestic, calm, or energetic according to the music chosen for their routine. Like circus horses, they often associate the music with particular movements.

Remember that your horse is a prisoner in its stall. You may enjoy having a radio playing while you work, but see whether your horse enjoys it as much as you do. Never leave a radio on all the time as it can really get on a horse's nerves, and be selective about the programs you tune in to, and the type of music played. The horse has to rely on you for both its entertainment and its peace and quiet.

LOVE CALLING!

Another experiment done at the Irish National Stud was that of playing the sound of a stallion calling to an in-season mare to study the effect this had on the brood mares stabled in a particular barn. It was found that those in season and ready to mate showed signs of being amenable to the stallion even though he was not present, and those not in season came into season after a very few days of the sound being played to them intermittently.

THE LANGUAGE OF EARS

The position of the ears is one of the most important indicators of a horse's mood and intentions. Ears pricked forward are a sign of alert curiosity and good mood. Ears turned back are often a sign of relaxation, or even boredom. They may also be a sign that the horse is unwell. Ears pressed flat against the head is a classic sign of bad temper and aggression. It can also signify that the horse is feeling stressed. When the ears flop to either side, it may be a sign of sleepiness or sickness. It is also a typical sign of submission to a more dominant horse.

Alert and interested

Relaxed, bored, or unwell

Sleepy, unwell, or submissive

Angry and aggressive

How Horses Communicate

Although they don't have a language, horses express themselves very clearly to other horses, and to humans who can understand their various facial expressions and general body language. Horses have, in addition, a very wide range of vocal sounds for expressing feelings, and possibly giving commands. Smell is also important among horses in understanding the status and condition of another horse, and sometimes of humans too.

Dominant or happy horses communicate this by making themselves look as big and impressive as possible. The head is up, the ears usually up and forward, the gait is prancing, and the tail is out and up. Submissive or unhappy (or sick) horses actually look smaller. The head is often down, the ears flopping sideways or held softly backward; it is listless or moves with no great energy or panache, and the tail is held low or even pressed down between the buttocks in fear.

It is important to be able to recognize the signs of anger in a horse, because an angry horse threatening to bite or kick can do serious injury. Its ears will be back, and it will have an angry expression in its eyes. The skin will appear to be drawn tightly on its face, the nostrils will be wrinkled up and back and the mouth may be open if it is thinking of biting. The tail may thrash about quite strongly (this alone is often seen in horses with a very dominant rider, particularly if they themselves are dominant horses who don't like being told what to do). If the horse is going to kick, or is

Above: Your relationship with your horse is as individual as those with your friends. It is impossible to say why two people, two horses, or a horse and a person hit it off and become friends; there is an intangible "chemistry" between the two.

warning that it may, a hind leg will be raised and the hoof waved about or carefully aimed.

If the horse you are riding behaves like this, it could simply be annoyed at being ridden, or at the general situation, or angry with a nearby horse (maybe an enemy), or irritated by uncomfortable tack or bad riding. You must work out which, because the horse can only communicate its displeasure, not describe what is annoying it. If riding near an angry horse, move away from it. If you are on the ground and handling a horse displaying these signs, be extremely careful to keep hold of its head (if you suspect a bite) and to keep away from its back legs (if you expect a kick).

Left: Horses are gregarious, social animals who live naturally in herds, associating closely with other herd members. Even in herds, however, they like to maintain a certain "personal space"; only foals with dams and close friends are regularly allowed to invade one another's space.

VOCAL CALLS

Horse sounds range from a soft whicker of affection from a mare to her foal, to a bloodcurdling scream from one stallion to a rival.

A neigh is a fairly loud, high, vibrating noise used to call to horses in the distance or to find out, by listening for an answering neigh, if there are any other horses nearby. A whinny is a softer, lower neigh given to greet a friend, equine or human, and may become excited and stronger when the horse is expecting food, or a stallion approaches a mare.

Squeals, short and sharp, can mean the horse has experienced a sudden pain, or can be an expression of play-feeling. Horses suffering from colic or laminitis often groan and grunt pitifully.

SMELLS

These are not consciously given off, but the smells a horse gives out are statements to others, although humans do not have a sufficiently sensitive sense of smell to recognize them. Mares in season, in particular, give off very specific scents to stallions, who recognize just when they are ready for mating.

When people are afraid they give off a specific smell which horses, at least, recognize easily. A horse may react by dominating its handler if it feels superior, or by becoming nervous if it is submissive.

Above: Rodeo horses like this bucking bronco are chosen for their propensity for bucking. A good deal of discomfort and mental distress are inflicted on these horses, and they cannot be blamed for hating the sight of humans.

MEETING A NEW HORSE

It is said that the first 30 seconds are vital when meeting someone new, and when meeting a horse for the first time the same holds true The wrong way to do it is to go straight up to the horse, pat it on the head and start ordering it around, tacking it up, or whatever. This is completely against the method horses use with each other, and you will succeed only in alienating it.

Speak the horse's name as you approach it slightly from one side. Stand a few paces away to let it look at you; then approach it calmly, with your arms down, and go close enough to let it smell you, as it would another horse. Let it take several seconds, then quietly raise your hand and stroke (not pat) the bottom of its neck, gradually working your way to its withers. Scratch it gently, talking quietly all the time and watching its reaction to you. Then, if you have a treat for it, give it your offering on the flat of your hand—and you may well end up with a friend for life.

RELATIONSHIPS WITH HUMANS

Horses are gregarious, social, herd animals, and as in most societies, there are bosses, followers, and in-betweeners in horse herds. The majority of horses are followers or in-betweeners and need human leadership from their trainers and handlers to feel settled and secure, and there is usually no need for very firm discipline with such animals. With dominant natural leaders the situation can be different, requiring firm (but not violent or cruel) handling from a skilled handler or trainer. However, if a dominant horse can be made to respect its handler and form a partnership it will often try its heart out for its rider, and some of the best competitive horse-and-rider teams have comprised such horses. Dominant horses recognize dominant humans. They only browbeat weak or bullying ones: the first type they dominate, as in nature, and the second they may well fight, again as in nature.

In the human world it is safest for a human, who understands the environment and circumstances, to be "boss."

The Points of the Horse

Conformation, or the make and shape of a horse, is a most important subject for anyone choosing a horse, especially if the horse has to compete or otherwise work hard.

UNDERSTANDING TERMS

A horse that is "short coupled" has a shortish back, and you cannot fit more than a hand's width between its last rib and the point of its hip. This makes for strength and handiness. "Slack loins" are the opposite of short coupled, indicating a rather long, weak back and possibly clumsy action.

"Well let-down" refers to the hocks, which should be "down near the ground": the lower part of the hind legs should be noticeably shorter than the upper part for more efficient leverage and less likelihood of tendon strain. The points of the hocks should be level with the front chestnuts when viewed from the sides. The front cannons should, similarly, be shorter than the forearm.

If a horse has a deep girth, it has plenty of depth and room for the heart and lungs. The length of the legs should not exceed the depth of the body from withers to breastbone.

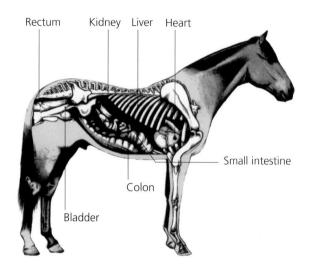

Above: Some of the horse's major organs. The horse's digestive system is specially adapted to deal with its natural diet of grass. The stomach is relatively small compared with that of a cow, and food is mainly broken down in the colon (large intestine), which is relatively large. Cellulose—the main component of grass—is broken down by the action of bacteria and digestive juices in this part of the digestive tract.

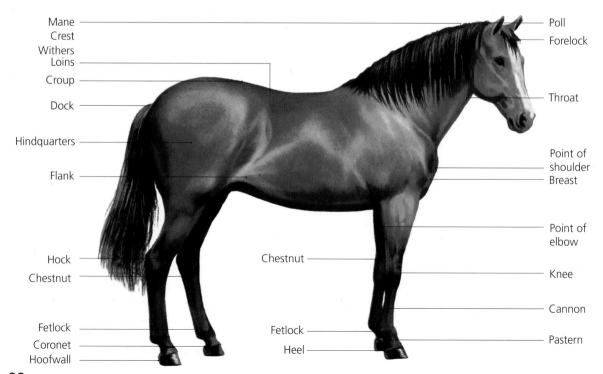

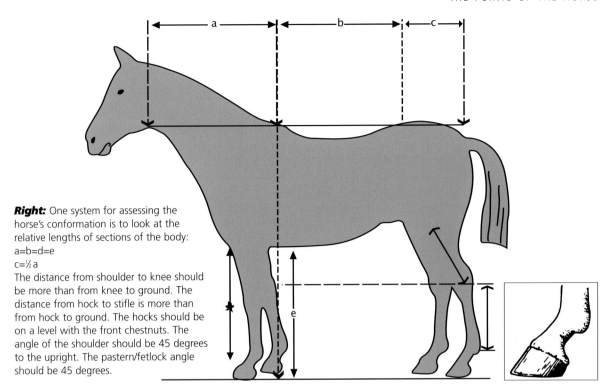

Right: One system for assessing the horse's conformation is to look at the relative lengths of sections of the body:
a=b=d=e
c=½ a
The distance from shoulder to knee should be more than from knee to ground. The distance from hock to stifle is more than from hock to ground. The hocks should be on a level with the front chestnuts. The angle of the shoulder should be 45 degrees to the upright. The pastern/fetlock angle should be 45 degrees.

If a horse has too-long legs, it is said to show a lot of daylight—in other words, a lot of space or daylight shows beneath its body. If it's short-legged and compact, it doesn't show much daylight—a good point.

Open elbows mean that you can fit your fist between the elbow and the ribcage, a very good point that should ensure a long reach (stride) with the forelegs so that the horse covers a lot of ground with each stride and therefore uses less energy.

Standing over a lot of ground means that the horse appears to stand squarely with a leg at each corner, rather than having its legs bunched together underneath it, which is a bad point.

GETTING YOUR EYE IN

The best way to imprint on your mind a picture of a well-conformed horse is to visit top-level shows and really study the top few horses in each class, noting the general proportions of the different points or areas of the horse. This takes time and practice, but by looking at the best and, after a few weeks, at those near the bottom of the line-up, you will be able to recognize good and bad conformation.

A horse described as "croup high" has the point of its croup higher than its withers. This is quite a bad point as the saddle will forever be sliding forward and digging in behind the shoulders, which can make the horse very sore and injure its muscles and skin. It also gives the rider an unpleasant "going downhill" feeling. The croup should be level with the withers or slightly lower for ordinary riding.

"Length of rein" refers to the distance between the horse's mouth and the rider's hand. A good length here provides the security of knowing that you have plenty in front of you, and are not likely to go over the horse's head too easily should it stop suddenly. Good length of rein depends on the horse having correctly proportioned neck and shoulders. If it has, it is described as having a good front. If not, it has a poor front or is short in front.

The shoulder of a riding horse should be well sloped, the horse being described as having sloping shoulders. The angle from the point of the shoulder to the point of the wither should be about 40 degrees or 45 degrees, and should be the same as the angle formed by the pasterns and feet with the ground. The hind feet and pastern angle (called the foot/pastern axis) can be slightly more upright. Pasterns that are too long and sloping can be weak, whereas upright pasterns make for an uncomfortable ride.

Colors and Markings

Coat color and markings developed over millions of years to give the horse the best possible camouflage for the area in which it lived. The more closely it resembled its background, the less likelihood there was of it being spotted by a predator.

One of the most primitive horse and pony colors is dun (a yellowy beige) with black points (the points being mane, forelock, tail, and the lower legs). In a woodland background or plains environment where by no means everything is a lush green, duns are extremely well camouflaged.

Below: Within these color categories there are different shades and varieties. If there is any doubt about the color of a horse, it is decided by the color of the points—the muzzle, tips of the ears, mane and tail, and lower part of the legs.

Old stories abound of good and bad colors in horses. Chestnut horses were supposedly hot-tempered, black horses nasty tempered and lacking in stamina, bay and brown horses dependable, and so on. The truth is that color has no bearing whatsoever on temperament or performance ability.

The only exceptions to this are horses that have pink skin under white hair (and some white-haired horses have dark skin underneath). These horses are much more susceptible to the weather than others, because pink skin lacks the strengthening substance melanin which is responsible for skin and hair color. The pink hue comes from blood circulating through colorless skin. Because this skin is less resistant to sun and wet, and hence bacteria, it is more susceptible to skin diseases, sunburn, and allergies.

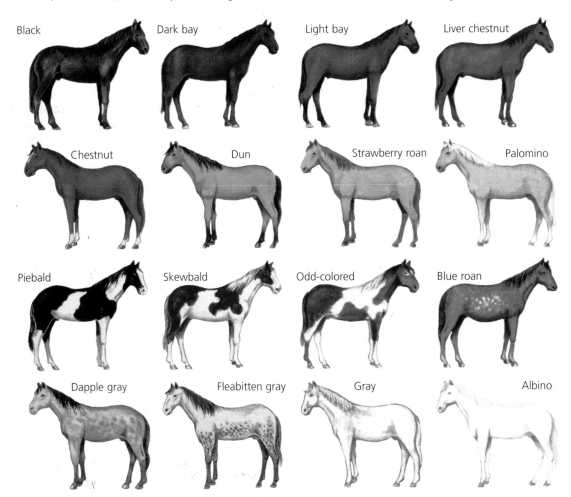

Black · Dark bay · Light bay · Liver chestnut

Chestnut · Dun · Strawberry roan · Palomino

Piebald · Skewbald · Odd-colored · Blue roan

Dapple gray · Fleabitten gray · Gray · Albino

Stripe

Blaze

White face

Snip

Star

The varieties of horse colors which abound today are the result of domesticated breeding, and bear no relation to camouflage. Some horses, such as palominos, paints, and pintos (piebalds, skewbalds, and odd-colored horses) are bred for special colors, and during the last century the German Royal Stud bred cremello (cream) horses for carriage-work.

Zebra marks, horizontal stripes found on the legs (darker than the coat color) and sometimes on the neck, withers, or quarters, are sometimes found on horses. Some pony breeds have a dark stripe running down the spine called a dorsal, or sometimes an eel, stripe. A few ponies and more donkeys have a further stripe running across this at the withers.

FOALS CHANGE COLOR

When foals lose their foal coat in their first fall it is quite common for them to change color; their adult color emerging underneath the fluffy foal hair as it falls out in patches. They look quite motheaten at this time. Chestnut foals will turn gray if they have one gray parent, and dun foals often turn bay.

ALBINOS

True albinos have no coloring agent in their bodies. They have pink skin, white hair, and pink eyes, like albino rabbits. Some so-called albinos have blue eyes, but this is not true albinism as blue is a coloring matter. Blue eyes are not all that common in horses, however; and where it does occur often only one eye is blue,

known as wall eye. There is no evidence that wall eyes see less well than dark eyes, but albinos with pink eyes (due to the blood circulating through an uncolored iris) are known to have poorer sight.

HEREDITY

Like all other characteristics, coat color is passed on by genes during mating. Some colors, such as bay and brown, are dominant (always shown in the coat), whereas others are recessive (they may not be shown in the coat, but are passed on as a "hidden" gene by a parent). Chestnut (sorrel) is recessive to all other colors—to be chestnut, a horse usually needs two chestnut parents.

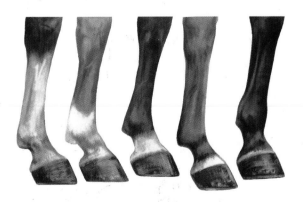

Above: White markings on the legs. From left to right: long sock, short sock, white pastern, short white pastern, coronet.

How the Horse Moves

The horse has four basic, natural gaits—the walk, the trot or jog, the canter or lope, and the gallop. However, there are other gaits which seem to come naturally to some breeds and are developed by man through selective breeding and training. These are, among others, the pace (most useful in harness-racers as it is faster than the trot), the tølt (in Icelandic ponies), and the gaits shown by American five-gaited saddle-horses: the normal walk, trot, and canter plus the slow gait and the rack.

The illustrations below show the footfalls in walk, trot, canter, and gallop. In basic training and competitive dressage, the first three gaits have four variations—collected, working, medium, and extended. Collected paces show maximum "gathering together" with great energy and impulsion, the horse happily flexing to the bit and showing no resistance. At the highest levels, the collected paces are often performed with a contact no heavier than the weight of the rein. Working paces are slightly longer in stride with no actual collection, the horse going contentedly "on the bit" (accepting and lightly holding the bit in its mouth, not leaning on, resisting or evading it). In medium paces the horse shows a more active, longer stride, and in the extended paces maximum stride length is achieved.

Below: The four basic gaits. The walk is the slowest and is a four-time gait in which all four feet hit the ground separately. The trot is a two-time gait; diagonal pairs of feet hitting the ground together. The canter is a three-time gait in which the horse can begin its stride with either hind leg, followed by the other hind leg and diagonal foreleg, and then the remaining foreleg. The gallop is a four-time gait. It is an extended version of the canter, except that all four feet hit the ground separately.

The actual tempo of a gait (the number of footfalls in a given length of time) should not increase as the horse changes from one version of a gait to another. The number of hoofbeats per minute in a working gait should be the same as in the extended form. In the extended gait, the stride is longer and more ground is covered in the given time; the horse does not move faster.

THE FOUR BASIC GAITS

The walk is described as a four-time gait, each footfall being clearly heard in a regular one-two-three-four sequence (although the natural walk is slightly irregular—one-two three-four). The trot is a two-time gait, one-two, one-two, with diagonal pairs of feet hitting the ground simultaneously and a suspension phase (when the horse is in the air) as it springs from one diagonal pair of legs to the other. The canter is a three-time gait—one-two-three, one-two-three—with the suspension phase after count three. The horse can begin its stride with either hind leg, followed by the other hind leg and opposite foreleg, and finish with the foreleg on the opposite side to the initial hind leg. The foreleg to land last is called the "leading leg" as the horse appears to point its direction with it as it canters. The gallop is a four-time gait, an extended version of the canter, but whereas in canter a diagonal pair of feet (say near hind and off fore) land together, in gallop they land separately, creating the four-time effect.

Walk

Trot

OTHER GAITS

The pace is a two-time gait, but whereas in trot diagonal pairs of legs move together, in the pace lateral pairs do so. The horse swings its off fore and off hind forward together, then near fore and near hind. The suspension phase is slightly longer than in trot, and a pacer can go as fast as a galloping horse.

The tølt is a fast amble (a lateral gait similar to the pace but slower and more broken in rhythm, making it a four-beat gait) used by Icelandic ponies as a comfortable, ground-covering stride.

The slow gait (also called by some the stepping pace or amble) is one of the paces of the five-gaited saddlebred, the footfalls being near hind, near fore, off hind, off fore. Peruvian Paso horses perform the same gait, and in them it is called the sobreandando. It is done under restraint in an energetic, showy way with the head up, chin in and steady or "set," and with knees and hocks greatly flexed and then extended, which contributes to the extravagant effect.

The rack is a flashy, fast walk with great flexing and lifting of the knees. It is very tiring for the horse, and the excessive leg movement stresses the forelegs and jars them considerably, making it suitable only for short periods on soft ground in the showring.

STRAIGHT AND TRUE

Most authorities like horses to move "straight and true"; in other words, they like the hind legs to follow in the same plane exactly behind the forelegs in every pace, straight from back to front with no sideways movement in normal gaits. This is certainly essential in dressage, and in most show horses. It is preferable in any performance horse in conventional competition such as eventing and show-jumping, as horses who "go crooked" (with their legs out of the alignment described above) are more likely to hit themselves in action, which can cause serious and repeated injuries.

HACKNEYS

Hackney horses and ponies have a very exaggerated gait in trot, where the forelegs are brought up flexed and high, and the hoof is "thrown" out in front with a cadenced (pausing-in-mid-air) effect that is very showy. The animal appears to be on springs, hardly touching the ground as it trots. The quality of this trot and the overall impression created by the gait play a large part in determining the winners in competition.

Canter

Gallop

Coat and Grooming

Horses and ponies grow two coats per year. The summer coat is short and sleek to allow for efficient heat loss in hot weather, when protection against cold and wet is not so critical; the winter coat is longer and thicker (because the longer hairs overlap), and protects the animal against wind by trapping a layer of warm air next to the body to insulate it, and against the wet. In native, cob, and cold-blood breeds, the winter coat has large numbers of longer hairs to help water drain off more efficiently. Such breeds also have long hair, called feathering, around the fetlocks to help protect against mud and wet.

Some pony breeds, particularly those from northern climes, have a double coat in winter, with long outer hairs to keep out the wind and rain, and shorter, softer under-hairs for extra warmth and protection. Their manes and tails are often very wiry and thick for the same reason.

The skin of all breeds produces natural grease to help lubricate the skin and hair and provide protection against the rain and, to a very small extent, flies. The skin itself has an outer layer of dead tissue which is gradually shed as fresh cells come to the surface to replace it. This outer layer ensures that the skin is protected and is not over-sensitive. The shed flakes are seen in an ungroomed animal's coat as dandruff.

In the natural state, this grease and dandruff does not become excessive, and is left on the skins and coats of domesticated horses that spend a lot of time at pasture, to help give protection. However, stabled animals have grease and dandruff removed by body brushing, to ensure that the skin is clean and stimulated, and able to work efficiently at excreting,

Above: Clipping helps to prevent excessive sweating and loss of condition during winter. The type of clip depends on the horse's workload, constitution, and how you keep it. The hunter clip (top) is only for very hard-working, stabled animals. The blanket clip (middle) suits moderate to hard-working horses stabled or kept on the combined system. The trace clip (bottom) is suitable for horses or hardy native ponies doing light work and kept outside.

Left: Rolling is one way in which horses groom themselves. It coats the skin and hair in dust or mud (which eventually dries). This helps to rid the skin of parasites, which cause great irritation to the horse and, by wounding the skin, can let in infection from bacteria and fungi. Rolling can also act like a dry shampoo, helping to remove excessive grease and dandruff.

through sweating, the waste products of exercise and a concentrated diet.

Horses groom themselves in the wild in a rough and ready way. Mutual grooming, where horses go along each other's back with the top teeth, helps dislodge and discourage parasites and is enjoyed by all. Horses also stimulate their skins by rubbing against hedges and trees, and by rolling.

ORDER OF GROOMING

First, with the long, stiff-bristled dandy brush, remove dried sweat, mud, and manure. Then body-brush all over, about six strokes in one spot, and using, where possible, long, firm, sweeping strokes, cleaning the brush with the metal curry comb every two or three strokes. Always brush backward and downward.

Push the mane hair over to the wrong side of the neck, then bring it back again with the body brush, a lock at a time, brushing right out from the roots to remove grease. To do the tail, grasp the end of the dock and the tail hair, holding the dock out toward you and horizontal to the ground. Let down one long lock at a time, brushing out the ends first and working up to the roots to get them clean.

Next, take one of two sponges (and never mix them up), wring out in warm water (although cold is refreshing in summer), and gently sponge away any discharge or dust from eyes, nostrils, and lips. Using the other sponge, do the sheath in a gelding or the udder in a mare, under the tail (dock) and between the buttocks. Dry with an old towel in cold weather.

Taking the water brush (a small, softer-bristled dandy brush), dip the tips of the bristles in water (not

the horse's drinking water), give a firm downward shake to remove the excess, and brush (or "lay") the hair of the mane, particularly at the roots on the crest of the neck, and the dock, to flatten the hair. You can give a final polish to the coat with a Turkish towel.

Above: The horse's hooves should be cleaned out each day. Marred dirt and straw can collect in the hoof and, if not removed, moisture will penetrate the hoof and may cause infection.

Above: As part of the daily grooming routine, the horse's eyes, nostrils, and lips should be cleaned with a sponge wrung out in warm water. These are sensitive areas, so be gentle.

CASTING THE COAT

Horses cast (change or molt) their coats in spring and fall and tend to look a little rough, particularly in fall. There is an old saying that no horse looks its best at blackberry time, and it's true. The hair comes out at intervals—the horse will cast a little and grow a little, cast a little and grow a little, until after a month or two the new coat will be complete, or "set."

Teeth and Hooves

Horses have particularly big, strong teeth—much more so in proportion to their size than humans—because their natural and domesticated foods are rough, tough, and need efficient mastication (chewing) to break them up and let in the digestive juices which process the nutrients so that they can be absorbed by the horse.

Domesticated horses need dental care to ensure efficient chewing and comfort in the mouth (discomfort being a major cause of head-shaking, bit resistance, and general bad behavior). The top jaw is wider than the bottom, so the chewing action wears the teeth on a slant. The outer edges of the top teeth and the inner edges of the bottom teeth (the back teeth or molars used for grinding up the food) can become very sharp, cutting into the cheeks and tongue respectively. Also, hooks can form on the front and back of the rows of molars that, if not removed, can result in the horse not being able to close its mouth.

The vet, or an equine dentist, can file or rasp off the sharp edges and hooks, and a horse may need this attention once or twice a year. Tartar may also form, particularly on older horses' teeth, causing gum disorders, and has to be scraped or chipped off.

MISSING TEETH

Teeth grow continuously, and if a tooth is removed or broken off, perhaps by a kick, its opposing tooth is no longer worn down constantly, and has to be regularly rasped down by the vet, otherwise it will interfere with the chewing action, and could grow into the gap and prevent the mouth from closing.

HOOVES

The horse's hooves are extremely complex structures, very sensitive to stress and pressure and with an excellent blood and nerve supply. On the outside and underneath, they are protected by horn (a form of

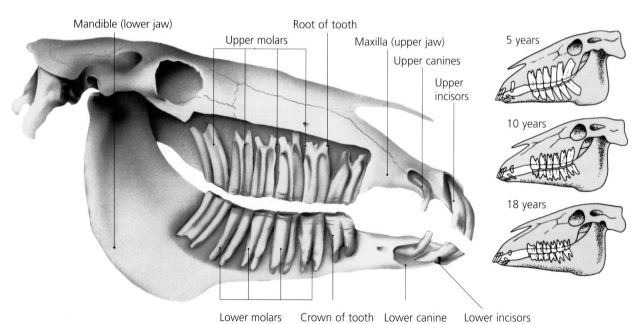

Mandible (lower jaw) Root of tooth
Upper molars   Maxilla (upper jaw)   5 years
                 Upper canines
                 Upper incisors   10 years
                                    18 years
Lower molars   Crown of tooth   Lower canine   Lower incisors

Above: A lengthwise section through a horse's skull. The incisor teeth at the front crop off the grass. The molars are very large, strong, grinding teeth. They need to be powerful to break down grass, which is tough and fibrous. The canines, or tushes, serve no useful purpose today, but are a throwback to a primitive ancestor.

Above right: The teeth continue to erupt from their sockets throughout the horse's life. The length of the crown in the gum shortens and the roots develop with age, and only a small amount of tooth is left by the time a horse becomes elderly.

modified, hardened skin) which grows down from the coronet band, a fleshy ridge around the top of the hoof, equivalent to the cuticle on human nails. Inside the hoof, the horny outer structures are tightly bonded to the sensitive ones by means of leaves of horn and flesh (called laminae) that interlock around the wall of the hoof. The sensitive structures themselves surround the bones of the foot.

When weight is put on the foot it flattens and expands slightly, squashing the sensitive tissues and their blood vessels between the horn outside and the bones inside. The blood is squeezed out up the leg into the veins, which have valves to keep the blood from running back again. When the weight is removed, fresh blood rushes back into the tiny vessels (called capillaries) and so the process goes on.

It was thought until very recently that it was almost entirely pressure on the frog that pumped the blood around like this, but recent research has shown that, although the frog plays a part, it is the expansion of the whole foot which is important. The frog, together with the plantar cushion inside the heels, mainly helps reduce concussion on the foot.

Below: As the teeth wear down throughout a horse's life, the pattern that can be seen on the surface of the incisors gradually changes, giving a fairly accurate idea of the horse's age. The teeth also become more triangular as a horse gets older, giving another clue to its age.

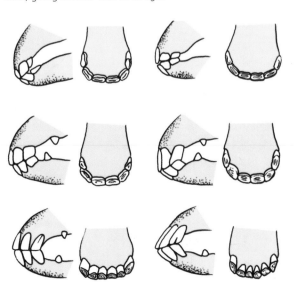

THE NEED FOR SHOES

The hoof horn grows all the time but is worn away very quickly in a horse working on a hard surface. Horses are shod with metal shoes to prevent them becoming footsore, but this stops the horn being worn down, so the farrier has to trim away excess horn at each shoeing before refitting or replacing the shoes (approximately every four to eight weeks, depending on the rate of wear and growth).

It takes a horse an average of six months to grow a complete new hoof. Existing horn quality cannot be improved. However, new horn can be improved by a diet containing methionine, biotin, and other substances, on which your vet can advise you.

Below: A cross-section through a horse's foot showing the outer layer of shock-absorbing horn surrounding the sensitive layers of tissue, and the bone structure of the foot.

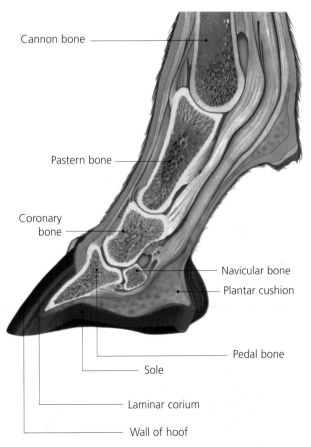

Cannon bone

Pastern bone

Coronary bone

Navicular bone

Plantar cushion

Pedal bone

Sole

Laminar corium

Wall of hoof

Breeding

Horse breeding can provide a great deal of satisfaction, but there are tremendous risks, not least financial ones. Commercial breeders expect mares to breed every year, with very few years off or barren, something which does not occur in the natural world. Stallions, also, cover mares many more times than they would in the wild.

Top stallions from any equestrian discipline, and especially flat-racing, are extremely expensive, and some are cosseted to the extent that they lead completely artificial lives with no natural contact with their mares, living in solitary confinement, turned out alone—although sometimes at least able to see other horses. It must be admitted that this often gives them warped personalities and bad tempers.

Those stallions allowed a more natural life and closer contact with other horses, spending a great deal of time out, perhaps with a quiet non-breeding pony mare for company, and particularly those allowed to run free with and mate their mares naturally, are better balanced mentally, and easier and safer to handle. They quickly learn to adapt to natural manners, and are often adept at avoiding kicks from mares not fully in season and unready to be mated. It has been shown many times that natural mating produces a much higher conception rate.

BREEDING CYCLES

Mares come into season in the spring and summer months as lengthening days, increasing warmth, and growing grass stimulate them to produce specific hormones (chemical messengers) to bring them into season and mating condition. These conditions produce a similar effect in the stallion, whose own hormones encourage the production of sperm ready for his mares coming into season. Breeders can bring their stock into breeding condition earlier in the year and extend the natural breeding season by blanketing up their animals, leaving lights on in the stables for longer on winter nights, increasing their feed, and sometimes by heating the stable buildings.

The mare will come into season at regular intervals of between 18 and 21 days, and will show her acceptance of the stallion (who can breed at any time) by standing with her hind legs straddled, tail raised and to one side, opening and closing the entrance to her vagina (called "winking"), and not resisting his advances. Mares not ready to mate, even though in season, will kick out.

PREGNANCY

After service (mating), if an egg has been fertilized the mare will "hold to service" (not come into season again) and the pregnancy should proceed. Blood and urine tests can inform the breeder whether or not the mare is pregnant, but even after confirmation, the

Right: The stallion's sexual organs consist of the penis, two testes in the scrotum which are linked by the spermatic cord to the prostate and bulbourethral glands, and the seminal vesicle. Sperm is produced in the testes and passes down the penis to meet up with the mare's egg. If mating is successful, a sperm will pierce an egg and fertilize it.

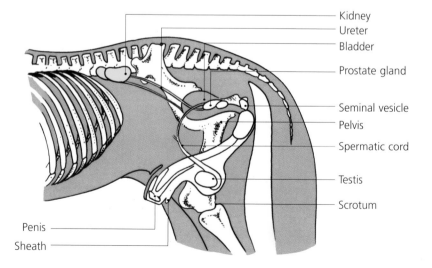

Kidney
Ureter
Bladder
Prostate gland
Seminal vesicle
Pelvis
Spermatic cord
Testis
Scrotum
Penis
Sheath

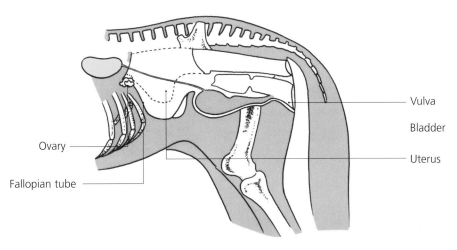

Right: The mare's sexual organs consist of ovaries, Fallopian tubes, uterus, cervix, vagina, and vulva. During the mare's sexual cycle eggs are released from the ovaries into the Fallopian tubes to meet up with the stallion's sperm and allow fertilization to occur.

Ovary

Fallopian tube

Vulva

Bladder

Uterus

Right: The breeding season of a mare normally lasts from March to October. During that time ovulation occurs every 18–21 days. She is at her most fertile in the two days before and after ovulation. If a mare is mated at this time, conception is likely. Pregnancy lasts about 11 months. The diagram shows the course of pregnancy of a mare mated in March.

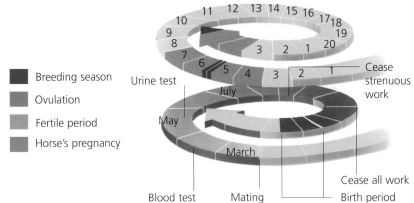

Breeding season
Ovulation
Fertile period
Horse's pregnancy

Urine test
July
May
March
Blood test
Mating
Cease strenuous work
Cease all work
Birth period

Below: In domestic conditions, the act of mating is often highly artificial, with the mare being restrained, sometimes with a foreleg strapped up, hobbled, or generally manhandled. It is said that this can prevent a valuable stallion being kicked and seriously injured. For her own protection, the mare may wear a sacking or leather neck cover as stallions often bite during ejaculation.

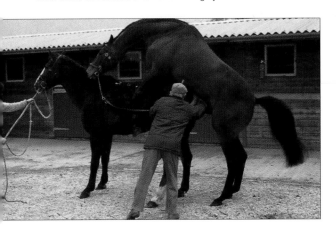

mare can lose the embryo (developing egg) and come into season again, necessitating another service. Ultrasound scanning is also now used in pregnancy detection.

The pregnancy lasts about 11 months. During the early months the mare can be ridden gently, and must not be overfed or restricted as this can adversely affect her health and that of her developing foal. For the last four months, the mare should nor be ridden and her diet should be increased in accordance with the vet's advice. As her time approaches, she will need more energy and protein but less bulk. She should be turned out so that she can exercise herself at will as this is essential to her health and that of the fetus (unborn foal) within her.

She must be kept calm and allowed the company of quiet, friendly horses, mares or geldings, who will not overexcite or annoy her. Separation from friends can cause anxiety and result in abortion.

Foalhood

Young foals should be correctly handled from birth — the sooner that they accept humans and learn commands, the sooner their behavior becomes instinctive to them, and the less difficulty there will be handling the growing, strong youngster, especially when breaking-in time comes. Well-handled foals are half backed already.

Formal lessons are not needed, but correct treatment, commands, and behavior should take place whenever you have anything to do with the foal. It is a great mistake to treat foals like puppies and play with them, however appealing they may be. They rapidly grow into mature, strong horses who then think it is acceptable to rear up and put their hooves on your shoulders or turn their quarters to you and play buck, asking to be scratched. No horse who behaves like this will find a ready market, and it can become dangerous to handle when the attitudes of humans toward it suddenly change, and it becomes confused.

All except foals of native types should come indoors at night during their first winter with their dams if they have not been weaned. Leaving them out will not toughen them up; rather, it will stunt them permanently as they will not be able to take in enough nourishment.

The old view of keeping foals and dams cooped up in their stalls for the first couple of weeks is wrong. Depending on the weather, it is important that they be turned out, into either a field or an indoor exercise

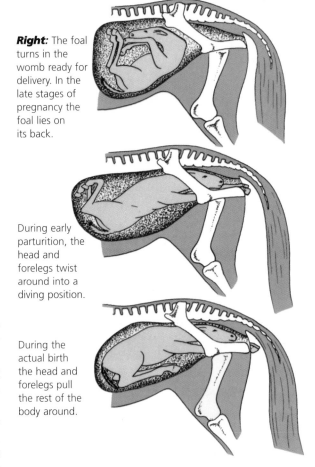

Right: The foal turns in the womb ready for delivery. In the late stages of pregnancy the foal lies on its back.

During early parturition, the head and forelegs twist around into a diving position.

During the actual birth the head and forelegs pull the rest of the body around.

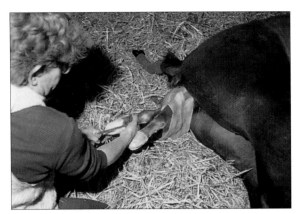

1 It is not usually necessary to help a mare, but in the event of delayed birth, unusual position of the foal, or other obvious problems, the veterinarian may be needed.

2 The foal is safely born and the mare licks it dry, absorbing its taste and smell. The foal also learns its dam's smell. They both lie and regain strength after the birth.

Above: If at all possible, foals should be turned out with other foals. It is better for their physical development and mental education to have other foals to play with. They will then form peer groups and learn herd manners.

area with a non-dusty flooring, after the first couple of days. This helps the mare gently recover from the birth and starts the foal off on the road to learning to use its legs and developing strong bones and muscles, and to learning what the world is all about.

At first mare and foal should be alone, but they should gradually be introduced to other mares and foals and kept in as natural a herd environment as possible. Foals will form peer groups and gangs, and learn herd manners—who is strong and who is weak; who is friendly and who is not.

FEEDING

For the first few weeks the foal will drink its dam's milk, but should be allowed to experiment with her concentrate feeds if it wishes. It cannot digest hay at this age. Gradually, as it eats more of her feed it should be fed concentrates of its own. It needs a high concentrate diet with plenty of protein and your veterinarian will advise on exactly what levels to feed. Gradually it will take hay and, of course grass, copying its dam and maybe spitting things out at first. All feed should be top quality and absolutely clean and there should be a permanent supply of water available.

WEANING

In nature weaning is so gradual it is barely noticed. Even mares with a new foal will be seen with last year's foal, now a yearling, tagging along taking the occasional suck, which does no harm.

In domesticity, foals are usually weaned at about six months of age. This can be a traumatic experience and leave lifelong mental scars if done too early or too suddenly. It's best to do it gradually, by introducing "nanny" mares to the herd and taking away the dams of the most advanced foals, who will soon attach to the substitute nanny mares. More and more mares are removed from the herd until the foals, over a period of a few weeks, are left only with the nannies, who give no milk.

Alternatively, the foals can be separated from their dams (and put together) for increasing lengths of time each day, until, after a few weeks, they are living separately.

3 Most experts believe it is best for the foal to struggle to its feet unaided as this is a vital learning process. If it has not stood up within an hour or two, gentle help can be given.

4 One day later, the mare and foal are doing well.

Health

Well cared-for horses remain in good health and your main contact with the vet should be for worming medicines, vaccinations, and an annual health check. However, there are a number of common illnesses and problems that occur even in the best managed establishments.

LAMENESS

Lameness is the most common complaint that horses suffer from. It can be caused by something simple like a stone in the foot, or by disease. Tendon injuries through strains or knocks are common, whereas problems such as wind galls (swellings on either side of the fetlocks) and degenerative joint disease (arthritis) are caused by wear and tear.

Laminitis occurs in ponies, cobs, and horses that are good doers (needing little feed to keep weight on) as its most common cause is overfeeding, although it can be caused by any blood disorder. Laminitis can result in the horse having to be destroyed, and you should call the vet immediately if you suspect your horse has it.

Navicular disease, which affects the navicular bone in the foot and is caused by excessive strain or jarring, can also cause chronic lameness.

RESPIRATORY PROBLEMS

Allergies are increasingly common in countries where horses are kept mainly in stables, and are due almost entirely to bad ventilation in stables. They give rise to a number of complaints, such as chronic obstructive pulmonary disease (COPD), formerly called broken wind. This is now known to be the result of an allergic reaction to mold spores, mites, or dust in feed or bedding, which cause damage to the lungs. The horse will have a harsh, dry cough and will have great difficulty breathing.

Influenza is a highly infectious disease which can permanently damage the lungs, and which needs a convalescence of several months.

Strangles is a diphtheria-like infection which, again, can cause permanent damage to the lungs and heart, and is very contagious.

Roaring, also known as laryngeal paralysis, is caused by wasting of the muscles around the windpipe. The nerves become damaged, causing paralysis and

Above: Rolling is one of the symptoms of colic. If a horse rolls and gets up without shaking itself, it could be feeling internal pain, and you should watch for other indications.

Below: Loss of hair can indicate a variety of skin complaints, such as saddle sores. They are often highly contagious and should be treated with strict attention to hygiene.

affecting the airflow to the lungs, and the horse makes a loud whistling noise when it exhales. Horses can also get sinus infections, coughs, and chills.

DIGESTIVE PROBLEMS

Colic accounts for the majority of digestive problems. The signs of colic are lethargy, loss of appetite, pawing the ground, and rolling. There are three types of colic: spasmodic, flatulent, and twisted gut. Colic can be caused by poor or irregular feeding, bad management, overeating, food which ferments very easily, stress, or, most common of all, worm damage.

Grass sickness is also a form of colic, in which the bowels become paralyzed.

Azoturia occurs when the horse is worked hard after being rested on a full working diet. The horse becomes stiff and unsteady and may reach the point of collapse.

Horses suffer from worm infestation, which causes loss of condition, and should be wormed regularly. Worms also cause diarrhea, as does too much grass.

SKIN DISEASES

Many skin diseases are contagious, so strict attention should be paid to hygiene when treating them.

Lice are common among horses, especially grass-kept horses in the spring. Sweet itch is caused by an allergy and affects the mane and tail. Ringworm is a fungal infection that can also be passed on to other animals and humans. Warbles cause a painful swelling on the back and are caused by the warble fly maggot. Skin allergies can be due to something the horse eats or to its bedding. Other skin diseases included mud fever, cracked heels, and nettle rash.

HEALTH CHECKS

Every horse, whether or not it is working, should have an annual veterinary check. For horses doing general riding and harness work, the vet will normally check the heart—listening to the rhythm of the heartbeat as well as the number of beats per minute. He or she will also assess the horse's lungs, looking for signs of congestion, possibly as a result of infection or allergy. Other checks will include looking at the condition of the hooves, eyes, and coat, and the way in which the horse moves—any stiffness could indicate arthritis.

Right: If a horse repeatedly rests the same leg, it can be an indication of lameness or injury to that leg or foot.

HORSE BREEDS

Breeds and Types

Ever since the horse first became domesticated, man has created specific breeds by selectively breeding from horses with different characteristics, to produce animals with the necessary physical and temperamental attributes to meet his own needs at the time. Many hundreds of breeds have been developed over the centuries, and they are constantly changing. Breeds die out because they are no longer needed. Draft and harness horses are an example of this; many of these breeds are now threatened. On the other hand, old breeds are altered, and new breeds are created, to meet new demands. The great increase in pleasure and competitive riding over the last twenty years has led to breeds being developed specifically for this.

A new breed is formally recognized when a stud book is opened. There are two types of stud book. New breeds usually have an open stud book; that is, the stallion and mare need not necessarily be of the same breed although both must be of pedigree stock. An open stud book allows for the continuing development of a breed, and for cross-breeding to correct any faults that might occur. Older breeds have a closed stud book, that is, both parents must be registered members of that breed.

CATEGORIES AND TYPES

Horse breeds fall into four categories: ponies, cold-bloods, warm-bloods, and hot-bloods. Pony breeds are defined as being under 14.2 hands. However, there are other differences between pony and horse breeds. Many pony breeds have developed in the wild and this has led to a natural cunning and hardiness that is not found in most horse breeds. They are seldom ill and rarely go lame. They have primitive features, and most breed true to type (the breed characteristics are reproduced consistently n the offspring). The cold-blood group consists of the heavy workhorses; they are gentle, docile, enduring, and hard-working. The hot-blood group contains the purebred Arab and Thoroughbred, who have fiery, proud, spirited temperaments. The warm-blood group is the largest

Below Left: A champion hunter showing the combination of strength and athleticism required of the type. Hunters are bred according to the type of country they will be working in. Many are crosses of Thoroughbred blood to give stamina and jumping ability, with heavier, sometimes native, breeds to give them calmness and endurance to carry a rider over difficult terrain all day.

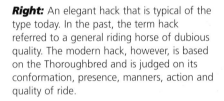

Right: An elegant hack that is typical of the type today. In the past, the term hack referred to a general riding horse of dubious quality. The modern hack, however, is based on the Thoroughbred and is judged on its conformation, presence, manners, action and quality of ride.

today. It contains all the sports and riding horse breeds, and some of the light draft breeds. These breeds have a mixture of ancestors. Most are descended from the Arab, but by crossing with draft or pony blood, horses have been produced that have spirit and stamina, are more robust than the Thoroughbred and Arab, and are tractable, responsive, and hardworking.

In addition, some categories of horse are not registered in any stud book, but they are recognized as specific types. The cob, the hack, and the hunter are examples of these types, although it is possible to have a registered Thoroughbred hunter or hack.

HACK

The term "hack" comes from the word hackney, or *haquenai*, which in medieval times referred to a hired horse of poor quality.

Gradually the term came to refer to a general riding horse, as opposed to a horse bred for hunting. There were two types of hack: the park hack and the covert hack. The park hack was ridden out for pleasure (hence the term "to hack," meaning to ride out) by the fashionable, and it therefore had to have good looks, excellent manners, and be an easy and comfortable ride. The covert hack was the horse that a gentleman rode to a foxhound meet while his groom took his hunter on at a more sedate pace. Again the covert hack had to be well-mannered and a comfortable ride.

Today hack refers to a top-quality riding horse for people who like to ride out and to look good. As well as having good manners and appearance, it must be well balanced, have a good action, respond well to the aids, and have the ability to jump small fences. In Europe, a small Thoroughbred type with a dash of Arab is popular as a hack, whereas in the USA the Saddlebred is favored.

Shows in different countries have different types of hack class. In the showring the hack is judged on conformation, presence, action, manners, training, and quality of ride.

HUNTER

The term "hunter" refers to a horse that is suited to carrying a rider behind foxhounds safely, sensibly, and comfortably for a season's hunting.

Different types of hunting country require different types of horses. In flattish country with large, open fields and big fences, speed and bold jumping are all-important, and Thoroughbred or near-Thoroughbred types are best. In rough or hilly country, or where the going is heavy, and where the scenting is less good, crosses of Thoroughbreds and light draft or native pony breeds are better as they provide a mount with a calm temperament, surefootedness, lots of stamina, and a good instinct for self-preservation.

Show hunters are divided into classes by weight. In Britain there are classes for heavyweight hunters capable of carrying over 196 lb (92 kg), middleweight hunters carrying 175–196 lb (82–92 kg), lightweight hunters carrying up to 175 lb (82 kg), small hunters between 14.2 and 15.2 hands, and ladies' hunters, which are to be ridden side-saddle. The qualities that are looked for are good conformation, good manners, an equable temperament, a comfortable ride, and good action in all paces, especially at the gallop. In the USA hunters are also divided into classes according to experience. In the USA, and in Britain's Working Hunter classes, horses are required to jump.

RIDING PONY

The riding pony type has been developed to provide a mount that is particularly suitable for children. The native breeds that evolved in the wild have many valuable qualities; they are intelligent, hardy, and surefooted. However, they are broad in the body, and can be very strong-willed, and it is commonly agreed that purebred native ponies do not necessarily provide the best type of pony for children. It has been the policy in many countries for some time now to cross

Below: Various breeds of riding pony have been developed in order to produce the ideal children's pony. The aim has been to combine the sturdiness, soundness, and kind temperament of the native pony with the class, speed, and athleticism of breeds such as the Arab. The Pony of the Americas, pictured here, produced in the 1960s by crossing a Shetland stallion and an Appaloosa mare, is a supreme example of the children's riding pony type.

Below: The cob type provides a stocky, sturdy riding horse. Cobs are produced from crosses, for example of heavyweight hunter and Thoroughbred, or Welsh Cob and Thoroughbred or Arab. They are bred to be strong, obedient, and placid, and they can carry a heavy rider all day. They are ideally suited to elderly or nervous riders.

the native breeds with Arab or Thoroughbred blood, to produce ponies that have good conformation, athleticism, elegance, and gentleness in addition to the character and sturdiness of the native pony.

Classes for riding ponies are held at shows in many countries around the world. Show ponies are divided into three classes: up to 12.2 hands, up to 13.2 hands, and up to 14.2 hands. These ponies are judged on conformation, manners, action, turn-out, and the performance of the rider, and ponies that contain a lot of Thoroughbred tend to do well. In working pony classes, competitors must also jump.

COB

The term cob refers to a distinct type of strong, stocky horse. Only the Welsh Cob is classified as a breed. They result from crosses such as a heavyweight hunter mare

with a Thoroughbred stallion, or a Welsh Cob mare with a Thoroughbred riding pony or an Arab stallion.

Cobs are compact and sturdy, obedient, and placid, and provide a very comfortable ride without too much speed. They are ideal for elderly and nervous riders, and for those who particularly need a horse with a calm temperament such as racehorse trainers supervising a string of young Thoroughbreds. Cobs are also immensely strong and can carry a heavy rider all day in the hunting field.

Classes are held for cobs at the majority of British shows. They are shown at the walk, trot, canter, and gallop; their action should be smooth, long-striding and comfortable, and they are judged on their ability to cover the ground in all paces.

In the past cobs were also popular harness-horses, but there is little demand for them in this role today.

Breeds of the World

Although many breeds of horse and pony originated in a specific place or a small region, they have now become widely dispersed around the world. They are listed here according to their country of origin. All the current major horse and pony breeds are included, and many less well-known ones are listed with their major founding breed. Information is given on the origins of each breed, the uses that they have been put to over the centuries, and what they are best suited for today. The development of each breed is described, showing why they developed in a particular way, according to the type of work that they were needed for at a particular period in history. Ancestry charts summarize the development of each breed by listing in chronological order the breeds that have contributed to it from its beginnings up until the 20th century. Fact boxes provide key information on the identification, characteristics, and principal uses of each breed.

NORTH AMERICA

Quarter-horse 60
Mustang 62
Morgan 63
Appaloosa 64
Standardbred 66
Saddlebred 68
Tennessee Walking Horse . .69
Palomino 70
Pinto 71
Pony of the Americas 72
Canadian Cutting Horse . .73

SOUTH AMERICA

Falabella 74
Criollo 75
Peruvian Paso 76
Paso Fino 77
Galiceno 78
Mangalarga 79

BRITAIN & IRELAND

Exmoor 80
Dartmoor 81
Fell 82
Dale 83
New Forest 84
Connemara 85
Shetland 86
Highland 87
Welsh Ponies 88
Cleveland Bay 90
Hackney 91
Shire 92
Suffolk Punch 93
Irish Draft 94
Irish Half-bred 95

WESTERN EUROPE

Anglo-Arab 96
French Trotter 97
Camargue 98
Percheron 100
Draft Breton 101
Friesian 102
Belgian Heavy Draft 103
Franches Montagnes 104
Trakehner 105
Hanoverian 106
Oldenburg 108
East Friesian 109
Holstein 110
Schleswig Heavy Draft . . .111
Lipizzaner 112
Haflinger 114
Gelderland 115

EASTERN EUROPE/ASIA

Tarpan 132
Konik 133
Wielkopolski 134
Kladruber 135
Shagya Arab 136
Furioso 137
Murakosi 138
Orlov Trotter 139
Don 140
Budyonny 141
Akhal Teké 142
Tersky 143
Karabakh 144
Vladimir Heavy Draft 145

SOUTHERN EUROPE	
Salerno	124
Italian Heavy Draft	125
Andalusian	126
Altér Real	128
Lusitano	129
Skyros	130
Bosnian	131

SCANDINAVIA	
Swedish Warm-blood	116
Swedish Ardennes	117
Fredericksborg	118
Knabstrup	119
Døle	120
Fjord	121
Finnish	122
Icelandic	123

MIDDLE EAST & AFRICA	
Barb	146
Caspian	147
Persian Arab	148
Basuto	149

ASIA & AUSTRALIA	
Manipur	150
Mongolian Wild Horse	151
Burma	152
Java	153
Sumba	154
Australian Stock Horse	155
Australian Pony	156
Brumby	157

Arab

The Arab is the oldest purebred horse in the world. Evidence suggests that it evolved from the group of prehistoric wild horses that spread across Asia to the Middle East. Rock paintings in southern Libya dating back 8,000 years illustrate a horse that looks remarkably similar to the modern Arab.

The Arab was captured and domesticated in several countries, and various strains have developed showing slight differences in size and appearance according to the local conditions. However, the horses of the Bedouin Arabs are the most famous, and the desert line is known as the Original or Elite Arab.

The Bedouins wanted horses that were tough enough to survive the harsh desert conditions and beautiful enough to be proud of, and they have selectively bred their horses for several centuries and possibly for as long as 2,000 years. Mares were chosen for their stamina and courage, and stallions for their beauty and intelligence. The Bedouins have always paid ruthless attention to purity of line; only asil (pure) horses could be bred into an asil line. The Bedouins inbred their horses in order to reinforce the breed's characteristics, unlike the Europeans, who have always believed that inbreeding creates weaknesses.

The Islamic religion was a major influence on the development of the breed. At the time when the Islamic empire began to expand in the eighth century, the prophet Mohammed realized the importance of having tough, fast, agile horses in battle. He instructed his followers to pay great attention to the

KEY FACTS

Color: Chestnut, bay, gray.
Height: 14.1–15 hands.
Physique: Small head, "dished" face, crested neck, long sloping shoulders, short back, deep girth, strong hindquarters, tail carried high and arched, hard clean leg, short cannon bone.
Character: Brave, intelligent, fiery, enduring.
Principal uses: Riding, improving other breeds.

care of their horses, and wrote that for each grain of barley that a man fed to his horse, he would be forgiven a sin in heaven.

The expansion of the Islamic empire brought the Arab to western Europe, where its superiority in battle over the heavy warhorses of the Europeans soon became apparent. Once the Moors had been driven

Left: This Arab displays the small head with dished face and thin muzzle, and the elegance and spirit that are characteristic of the breed. Due to its close association with humans over the centuries, it enjoys human companionship and is quick to learn.

ANCESTRY

Asiatic
wild stock

Arab

out of Spain, the Arab horses that were left behind were crossed with native horses to produce a new type of battle horse, the Andalusian, that was still large and powerful, yet also fast and very agile. The Arab's reputation for stamina, speed, and agility quickly spread, and it was soon in demand throughout Europe for cross-breeding with local horses.

The Arab's ability to stamp its conformation soundness, its free, floating action, stamina, and gentle nature on all its offspring have made it very popular for founding and refining other breeds, with the result that it has had more influence on the world's horse population than any other breed. All warm-blood breeds contain Arab blood, as do many pony breeds, and even a few of the cold-blood breeds.

The Arab is still as popular as ever and Arab breeding farms exist in countries all over the world. However, there is a danger that indiscriminate breeding in order to supply this demand could lead to a deterioration.

In addition to being popular for cross-breeding, the Arab makes a good riding horse. And although the purebred Arab is not used for showjumping or eventing, it is ideally suited to competitive events like endurance riding.

Below: An Arab foal with its mother. The Arab has the capacity to stamp its qualities on all its offspring, and is in as much demand as ever around the world for founding and improving other breeds. The purity of the breed is jealously guarded by Arab horse societies in many countries.

Thoroughbred

KEY FACTS

Color: Most solid colors.

Height: From 14.2–17.2 hands, depending on purpose: average about 16 hands.

Physique: Varies; refined head, long arched neck, sloping shoulders, deep chest, short strong back, deep body, muscular hindquarters, hard legs.

Character: Bold, spirited.

Principal uses: Racing, riding, cross-breeding.

The Thoroughbred is famous the world over as the racehorse par excellence. It is the fastest, and the most valuable, horse in the world. However, it did not emerge as a breed until relatively recently.

Horseracing, which had always been popular in England, reached new heights of popularity during the reign of Charles II. The fastest of the native mares, which probably included the now extinct Galloway Ponies, had for some time been crossed with imported Arabs, Barbs, and Turks, in order to improve the speed and performance of these "running horses," and gradually a better class of racehorse was emerging.

Although many Arab stallions were being used at this time, three in particular were very influential. The first to arrive in England was the Byerly Turk, which was put to stud in 1690. Next was the Darley Arabian, which arrived in 1704. Darley Arabian was the great-

ANCESTRY

Arab

Turk

Barb

Galloway

Thoroughbred

grandsire of Eclipse, the most famous racehorse of all time. Darley Arabian also sired Flying Childers, who was never beaten. The last was the Godolphin Arabian, which arrived in 1728.

These stallions were crossed with the best of the English racing mares so successfully that all Thoroughbreds registered in the General Stud Book, started in 1791, can be traced back to them.

As horseracing developed into an industry, breeders began to pay great attention to pedigree, and to use only horses that had proved themselves on the racetrack. In the beginning, Thoroughbreds were raced over long distances of about four to 12 miles (6.4 to 19.3 km), but gradually demand grew for shorter races so that horses could be raced at a younger age. They became better fed and looked after, and as a result the breed became taller and faster, until it reached its peak in about 1850.

Foreign interest in the Thoroughbred has always been strong, and it has been exported in large numbers. It is now bred all over the world, and several countries are famous for producing top-class horses. In particular, the United States is known for its outstanding young sprinters, and France for its middle-distance horses and stayers. Ireland also breeds consistently top-class Thoroughbreds.

The Thoroughbred, with its good conformation, long, easy action, and good balance, also provides a

TYPES OF THOROUGHBRED

Thoroughbreds are divided into those that race on the flat and those that race over jumps.

There are three categories of flat racers: the sprinters, which race over a distance of 5–7 furlongs (1,100–1,590 yd/1,000–1,450 m)—these are young horses that mature early, and have a lot of speed but little stamina; middle-distance horses, which race over the "classic" distances of 1–1¾ miles (1.6–2.8 km), such as the Kentucky and Epsom Derbies; and the stayers; late-maturing horses that race over longer distances.

Those that race over jumps are divided into steeplechasers and hurdlers. They require toughness, stamina, and jumping ability.

Horses are bred for a specific category, as each has a different requirements.

perfect riding horse. Crossed with horses with a calmer temperament, it produces excellent show-jumpers, event horses, and hunters and it has been used in the creation or development of many modern breeds of sports horses, such as the Anglo-Arab, the Trakehner, and the Westphalian.

Below: Thoroughbred racing at Happy Valley, California. The United States is famous for producing outstanding young sprinters. The Thoroughbred breed has evolved over the last 200 years into the foremost racing horse in the world. Today it is raced in over 50 countries.

Quarter-horse

The Quarter-horse is the oldest surviving American horse breed, although it was not officially recognized as a breed until 1941.

In the 17th century, on Sundays and holidays, the settlers of Virginia and the Carolinas used to enjoy racing their horses down the main street of the local town—usually a distance of about a quarter of a mile (0.4 km). Horses that had been bred by crossing local Chicasaw Indian ponies (mustangs of Arab, Barb, and Turk origins) with Thoroughbreds imported from England proved extremely fast over this distance, and were soon in demand as breeding stock. Among these, a stallion called Janus, imported from England in 1756, is recognized as the foundation stallion of the breed. Janus had raced over four miles in England; however, his offspring were very successful over a quarter-mile.

Soon the Quarter-horse was being carefully bred to produce a very fast horse with great powers of acceleration for sprint racing. With the development of Thoroughbred racing, quarter-mile racing also became more organized and more popular.

The breed quickly came to be valued for other qualities as well as its speed. It is a tremendously strong horse with very powerful shoulders and hindquarters, and it was able to carry heavy men and packs for long distances. It is able to make quick starts and tight turns, which make it the perfect horse for roping and cutting work with cattle. In addition it seemed to have a good instinct for cattle-work. It was taken west with the pioneers, and proved to be the ideal horse for working on the big ranches that were springing up across the country.

The modern Quarter-horse combines strength, speed, and agility with intelligence, and is also easily broken and handled, making it extremely popular. There are different types of Quarter-horse depending on what type of work they have been for, but they all share the same Quarter-horse qualities. The heavier type is produced for stock-work, and a lighter type for racing. To see a cutting horse at work, springing into a gallop from a standing start, skidding to a halt, and turning on a sixpence, is an exhilarating spectacle. Working cattle, it moves fast and low, anticipating every move that the calf makes.

The versatility of the Quarter-horse is illustrated by the many types of class in which it is shown, such as working classes, jumping, hunting, and polo classes. It is also successful in open classes against other breeds.

The Quarter-horse is the most numerous breed in the United States today, with two million registered there. Its popularity has led to it being exported all over the world, and a further 800,000 are registered worldwide. It is now bred in Canada, South America, Australia, England, and South Africa.

Below: The Quarter-horse's powerful hindquarters enable it to move fast and low when it is working with cattle, starting and stopping suddenly and making tight turns. It is also kind, willing, docile, and intelligent, and is the most popular horse breed in the United States today.

THE RACING QUARTER-HORSE

The Quarter-horse, named after the distance over which it excels, is still bred for racing, and the richest horserace in the world is the All American Futurity for three-year-old Quarter-horses.

Despite the challenge provided by the Thoroughbred, the Quarter-horse is still the fastest horse in the world over a quarter-mile (0.4 km), the current record being around 20 seconds.

Above: Dash For Cash, the top money-winning Quarter-horse in the US. Quarter-horse racing has retained its popularity in the US despite the emergence of the Thoroughbred.

KEY FACTS

Color: Solid colors, usually chestnut.
Height: 14.3–15.1 hands.
Physique: Short head, muscular neck, short-coupled body, broad powerful hindquarters, fine legs.
Character: Intelligent, versatile.
Principal uses: Riding, ranch-work, rodeos, racing.

ANCESTRY

Arab

Barb

Turk

Andalusian

Thoroughbred

Quarter-horse

Mustang

The Mustang is the feral horse of North America, descended from the horses of the Spanish settlers, and therefore of Andalusian, Arab, and Barb origins. Mustangs roamed free for over 300 years, during which time they developed into hardy, thrifty, independent horses. Many were caught by the Indians, and later they were popular with the cowboys. Early Mustangs showed their Spanish and Barb origins, but many of the best were captured and the quality of the herds left in the wild declined.

The Mustang was found to have good cow-sense and, as well as being used for cattle-work, it was crossed with other larger breeds brought over by the early settlers to create larger working horses, and later with the Thoroughbred. The Quarter-horse was the outstanding breed produced from the Mustang, and it was also influential in the development of the other stock breeds, the Appaloosa, Palomino, and Pinto.

Today the wild Mustang has declined in numbers and is protected by law. In addition, various registries have been established to preserve the different bloodlines. The Spanish Mustang Registry is for horses of obvious Barb descent. These horses are very good for general and endurance riding. The Spanish Barb Mustang Registry is for horses that are not of pure Barb descent but which still show the correct characteristics. There is also an American Mustang Association.

KEY FACTS

Color: All colors.
Height: 14–15 hands.
Physique: Varies; lightweight build, hard legs and feet.
Character: Independent, intractable.
Principal uses: Stock-work, riding, endurance riding.

ANCESTRY

Andalusian
Arab
Barb
Turk

Mustang

Morgan

ANCESTRY

Welsh Cob
Thoroughbred
Native stock

Morgan

The Morgan is the first American breed. It was founded from a single stallion called Figure, foaled in Massachusetts in 1793, which eventually came to be named after one of its owners, Justin Morgan of Vermont. The origins of this stallion are unknown, but it is thought to be a combination of Welsh cob, Thoroughbred, and native stock of Arab and Barb descent. Justin Morgan (the horse) excelled at both saddle and harness racing, and at pulling heavy weights, as well as being a good riding and ranch horse, and he was in great demand as a sire. He stamped his size, conformation, and character on his offspring with such consistency that by the time of his death in 1821 a new breed had been created.

During the 19th century the Morgan was itself used in the foundation of other great American breeds, including the Standardbred, the Saddlebred, and the Tennessee Walking Horse.

In the past the Morgan was used mainly for ranch and harness work, and proved its strength by doing heavy draft work. However, it is now also frequently used as a saddle horse.

With its strength and stamina, elegant highstepping action, and good nature, the Morgan is still popular today. It makes an ideal family horse as it takes easily to any form of equestrian activity, be it pleasure riding, endurance riding, or showing in harness.

KEY FACTS

Color: Predominantly bay; also brown, black, chestnut.
Height: 14–15 hands.
Physique: Medium-sized head, slightly concave face, thick neck, deep chest, broad back, muscular quarters and highset tail, legs set square.
Character: Good-natured, hard-working, active.
Principal uses: General riding, harness work.

Appaloosa

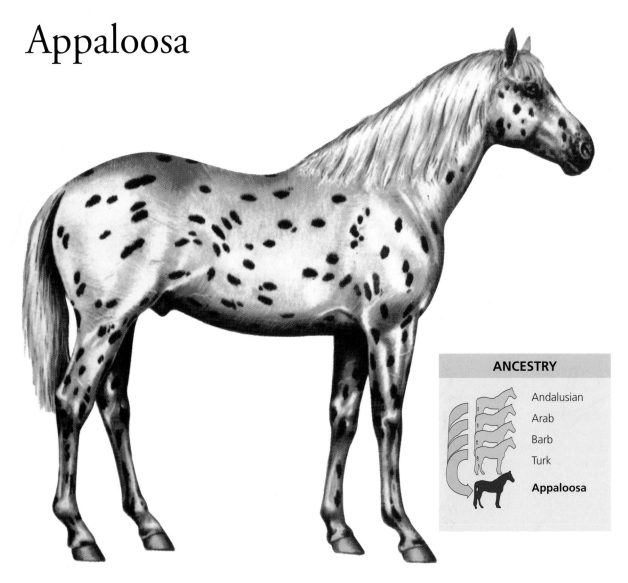

ANCESTRY

Andalusian

Arab

Barb

Turk

Appaloosa

From the evidence of early cave paintings such as those as Lascaux, it appears that spotted horses existed as far back as prehistoric times. They are known to have existed in ancient Persia, and in China, and they appear again in Egyptian art. Spotted horses, probably descended from those of ancient Persia, were bred in Spain from about AD 100, and developed into a fine riding horse.

These horses were amongst those taken by the Spanish Conquistadors to Mexico in the 16th century, and are presumed to have escaped and spread across North America. The Nez Perce Indians of north-western America (now Washington, Oregon, and Idaho) were skilled at horse-breeding, and from these escaped horses they produced spotted horses that

were fast, strong, and agile to cope with the mountainous terrain of the region, yet also docile and easy to handle. The Nez Perce Indians lived near the Palouse River and the breed came to be known as the A Palouse, and later the Appaloosa.

In 1877 the Nez Perce tribe was nearly destroyed by the US army. However, their horses were captured, and subsequent careful breeding has produced a spotted horse that in 1938 was recognized as a distinct breed. Although it is still found mainly in the western part of the country, it is now among the half-dozen most popular breeds in North America.

There are six main Appaloosa patterns, but no two horses are exactly the same. Leopard consists of an all-over white background with dark spots. Snowflake consists of an all-over dark background with white spots. Spotted Blanket consists of a mainly dark body, with dark spots on white back and/or hindquarters. White Blanket consists of a mainly light body with dark back and/or hindquarters. Marble consists of a dark coat at birth that fades almost to white as the horse grows older, except for a few darker markings on legs and face. Frosted Tip consists of a dark background with light-colored or white spots on loins and hips. There are several pattern variations. Roan is the most common ground color, although any color is acceptable, as long as the pattern conforms to an accepted one.

The Appaloosa has a smooth action and is tractable in character, making it popular as a general riding horse, and for trail-riding, driving, and ranchwork. It is admired around the world for its distinctive appearance, and it is also in demand for shows and circuses.

Spotted horses and ponies exist all over the world. However, they are a breed, not a type, and they should not be confused with the Appaloosa.

KEY FACTS

Color: Six basic color patterns—Frost, Leopard, Snowflake, Marble, Spotted Blanket, and White Blanket.
Height: 14.2–15.2 hands.
Physique: Short-coupled, thin mane and tail, hard feet which are often striped.
Character: Courageous, docile.
Principal uses: Pleasure riding, cow pony, parade and circus horse.

Below and below right: Six main Appaloosa patterns are recognized. The Appaloosa can be any color, but the markings must conform to one of these six patterns, such as the Leopard pattern (below) and the Spotted Blanket (below right).

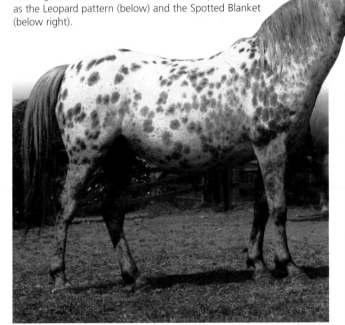

Standardbred

KEY FACTS

Color: Any solid color.

Height: 14—16 hands.

Physique: Conformation varies; Thoroughbred-type, but heavier.

Character: Courageous, calm temperament.

Principal uses: Harness-racing.

In the middle of the 19th century, cross-breeding produced one of America's greatest breeds, the Standardbred, which today is the fastest harness-racing horse in the world.

The breed can be traced back to a Thoroughbred stallion called Messenger which was imported to the United States in 1788. Harness-racing was popular at that time, but it was an amateur affair, and no thought had been given to founding a breed of trotters. However, when Messenger was crossed with the fastest of the local harness-racers, horses resulted that had exceptional trotting speed. He sired four sons to which almost all Standardbreds can be traced. As

ANCESTRY

Thoroughbred

Canadian Trotter

Hackney

Narrangansett Pacer

Arab

Barb

Morgan

Standardbred

harness-racing became more popular during the 19th century, selective breeding was practiced to produce faster trotters. Thoroughbreds were crossed with more robust strains that had a talent for trotting, such as Canadian Trotters, Hackneys, Narragansett Pacers, horses of Arab and Barb origins, and Morgans.

The most famous and successful of Messenger's descendants, his great-grandson Hambletonian 10, born in 1849, sired over 1,300 offspring. He is regarded as the father of the modern Standardbred.

Harness-racing is divided into trotting and pacing. In both, the horse pulls a sulky (a light, two-wheeled vehicle) and is guided by a driver. Trotters move diagonally, in a conventional trot. Pacers move laterally, that is, the legs on the same side move together. Pacing is a natural gait, and horses born with a talent for pacing are trained for it from an early age. Many pacers wear hobbles, which synchronize their strides and prevent them from breaking the trot.

In 1871 the American Trotting Register was founded, and in 1879 a standard was laid down for inclusion in it. Over a distance of 1 mile (1.6 km) trotters had to attain a time of 2 minutes 30 seconds, and pacers a time of 2 minutes 25 seconds. It is from this standard that the breed takes its name.

Harness-racing is a popular sport in many countries around the world, and it is found in Australia, New Zealand, South Africa, and several European countries such as Sweden, Germany, France, and Russia. It has been used to improve many trotting breeds, including the German Trotter, the French Trotter, and the Orlov Trotter.

The Standardbred's conformation varies, as it has been bred primarily for speed. It resembles the Thoroughbred, but is heavier and more robust, and has very strong hindquarters. Although predominantly a harness-racing horse, the Standardbred's speed and stamina, keenness, and calm temperament make it excellent for general riding. Its qualities also suit it to endurance riding.

BREAKING THE RECORD

In 1871 the standard for the breed was set: one mile (1.6 km) in 2 minutes 30 seconds for trotters, and 2 minutes 25 seconds for pacers. Yet this time had already been bettered in 1845, when one mile was trotted in 2 minutes 29½ seconds by a mare owned by Lady Suffolk. Nearly 100 years later, in 1938 the record stood at 1 mile trotted in 1 minute 55¼ seconds by a gelding called Grayhound. Recently the time for a trotter fell to 1 minute 54⅕ seconds.

Pacers are even faster than trotters, and the fastest recorded time over one mile by a pacer, achieved by a horse called Steady Star, is 1 minute 52 seconds, the equivalent of 32 mph (51 km/h).

Above: A pacer performing at Palm Beach, Florida. A pacer moves with lateral rather than diagonal strides, and can go slightly faster than a trotter. Horses with a natural inclination to pace are trained to it from an early age.

Saddlebred

The saddlebred was developed in Kentucky during the 19th century by plantation owners, who were looking for a horse that provided a comfortable ride for plantation work combined with a stylish, eye-catching action in harness. By crossing the best of their original stock of Thoroughbreds, Morgans, and Narragansett Pacers, they produced a horse that was intelligent and responsive and which also had speed and stamina. With its high head-carriage and high-stepping action, it is extremely elegant.

Intensive breeding has enhanced the Saddlebred's conformation and action, and it is now a very popular and successful showhorse. The breed is divided into three divisions for showing. The Three-gaited horse is shown in the three natural gaits. The Five-gaited horse is shown in the three natural gaits and two manmade gaits: the slow gait and the rack. The slow gait is a very slow, smooth, four-beat movement. The legs, especially in front, are lifted very high. The rack is a fast version of the slow gait requiring a very snappy knee and hock action. The Fine Harness horse is shown with a four-wheel vehicle and is judged in two gaits: an animated walk, and an airy part-trot.

Although it is best known as a showhorse, the Saddlebred also makes a good general riding and driving horse.

KEY FACTS

Color: Black, brown, bay, gray, chestnut.
Height: 15–16 hands.
Physique: Narrow, refined head, large eyes, long elegant neck, sloping shoulders, short body, strong flexible hindquarters, long fine legs, high head and tail carriage.
Character: Intelligent, gentle.
Principal uses: Riding and showing.

ANCESTRY

Thoroughbred

Morgan

Narrangansett Pacer

Saddlebred

Tennessee Walking Horse

The Tennessee Walking Horse (the Walker for short) was developed from the Thoroughbreds, Morgans, Standardbreds, Saddlebreds, and Narragansett Pacers owned by the Tennessee settlers in the 18th century. Crosses of these led to the foundation stock of the modern breed.

In the beginning the Walker was intended as a general-purpose working horse, but its extreme comfort as a riding horse made it very popular with the owners of the vast southern plantations.

The Walker's conformation is unique. It has a compact and powerful frame. Its forelegs are set slightly apart, and its hindlegs are set with the hocks well away from its body. Its gaits—the flatfoot walk, running walk, and canter—have been developed specifically to produce a very smooth ride, and cannot be taught to any other breed. The flatfoot walk consists of a smooth, gliding action as the horse "floats" over the ground, its hind feet overstriding the front by 12–20 in (30–50 cm). The running walk is a faster version of this gait, in which the horse achieves great elevation, and can sustain a speed of up to 15 mph (24 km/h). In the canter it elevates its forehand with a rolling motion while its hindquarters remain almost level. The running walk is now inbred; foals are seen performing it just by copying their dams.

KEY FACTS

Color: Chestnut, black, bay, roan; white markings common.
Height: 15–16 hands.
Physique: Straight profile, long powerful neck, sloping shoulders and broad chest, short back, strong sloping hindquarters, fine legs, profuse tail carried high.
Character: Docile, willing.
Principal uses: Riding and showing.

ANCESTRY

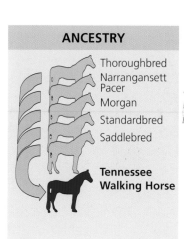

Thoroughbred
Narrangansett Pacer
Morgan
Standardbred
Saddlebred

Tennessee Walking Horse

Palomino

The distinctive and beautiful color of the Palomino has made it popular all over the world. It is defined by its color rather than its conformation, and as it does not breed true to type, it is not recognized as a breed except in the United States. Elsewhere it is registered as a type, and Palomino societies and stud books exist.

The Palomino's origins are believed to go back to ancient China, where the early emperors are reputed to have ridden golden horses. However, they reached America from Spain along with the early Spanish settlers. When the Spanish were defeated and their horses escaped, the Palominos gradually joined up with the herds of wild mustangs roaming North America. Later, they were picked out from these herds of wild horses, and became a popular mount of the cowboys.

The color of the Palomino should be that of a newly-minted gold coin, although in the United States slightly lighter and darker shades are also allowed. The mane should be white.

In North America the Palomino has been bred as a quality riding horse, and is used extensively for trail riding, stock work, and rodeos. In Britain, Palomino ponies are popular mounts for children.

The Albino is another color type that is recognized in the United States, where it has been bred since the early 20th century. It is probably descended from an Arab–Morgan stallion, and has bred true to type over several generations.

KEY FACTS

Color: Gold, with light mane and tail; white markings allowed on legs.
Height: Varies; usually over 14 hands.
Physique: Varies; should be of riding horse/pony type.
Character: Varies.
Principal uses: Pleasure and trail riding, ranch work, rodeos.

ANCESTRY

Mustang

Palomino

Pinto

KEY FACTS

Color: Black with white, or white with any color except black.
Height: Varies.
Physique: Varies.
Character: Varies.
Principal uses: Pleasure riding, ranch work, showing.

This spectacularly colored horse was traditionally associated with the American Indians. However, today it is popular for general pleasure riding and showing. Like the Palomino, the Pinto was originally registered as a color.

Pinto coloring falls into two types. "Overo" coloring consists of large bold patches of black with white. "Tobiano" coloring consists of white with smaller patches of any other color except black.

Today, three registers cover the Pinto in the United States, relating to different categories of conformation. The American Paint Horse Registry covers the Stock Horse type, for horses originally of Quarter-horse or Thoroughbred breeding and conformation. The association is dedicated to upgrading the Paint Horse, and to qualify horses must be of either Paint Horse, Quarter-horse, or Thoroughbred parentage. The Pinto Registry covers Pinto-colored horses of all breeds and types and has three divisions: the Stock Horse type; the Hunter type, an English horse of Arabian or Morgan origins; and the Saddle type, also an English horse, of Saddlebred origins. The Moroccan Spotted Horse Association covers gaited horses, such as those of Hackney, Tennessee Walking Horse, Morgan, and Thoroughbred origins.

ANCESTRY

Mustang

Pinto

Pony of the Americas

The Pony of the Americas was the first pony breed to be developed in the United States. It is of recent origin, having been developed in the 1950s by Leslie Boomhower of Mason City, Iowa. He crossed a Shetland stallion with an Appaloosa mare, and the result was an attractive miniature Appaloosa colt. The colt proved so popular and successful in the showring that it was used to found a new breed.

The breed's popularity has grown fast; it already has its own stud book, and numerous POA clubs have been founded across the United States and Canada. Although foals can be included provisionally in the stud book, it is not until a pony is three years old that it can be officially registered. Entry is on the basis of height, type, and coloring.

The pony has long strides and a good, free action. It provides an excellent mount for young riders, being ideal for general riding, trail riding, showjumping and racing.

KEY FACTS

Color: Appaloosa colors and patterns.
Height: 11.2–13.2 hands.
Physique: Arab-type head, good shoulders, deep chest, short back, rounded body, strong hindquarters, clean legs.
Character: Willing, versatile.
Principal uses: Children's riding pony.

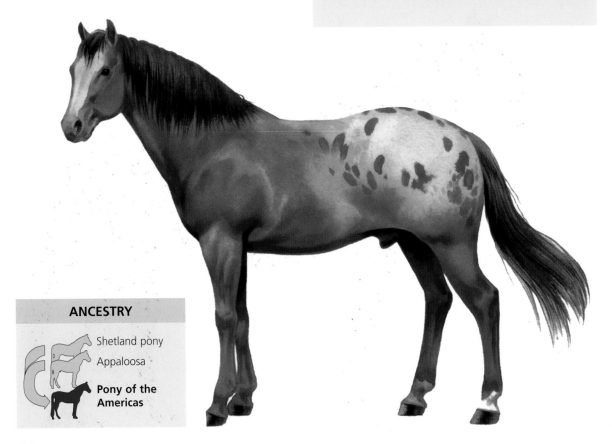

ANCESTRY

Shetland pony
Appaloosa
Pony of the Americas

Canadian Cutting Horse

Color: Any color.
Height: 15.2–16.1 hands.
Physique: Like the American Quarter-horse; long body, short legs, powerful hindquarters.
Character: Intelligent, easy to break.
Principal uses: Ranch work.

Above: Somewhat larger than the Quarter-horse, the Canadian Cutting Horse has similar qualities of agility and endurance.

Canada has no native horse breeds (although it does have a native pony, the Sable Island Pony).

However, horse breeding has been carried out from imported stock since the first settlers arrived. One product of this is the Canadian Cutting Horse, which has been developed along the lines of the Quarter-horse. It is exceptionally strong, fast, and agile and, like the Quarter-horse, is ideally suited to working with cattle. However, it is not yet recognized as a breed, only as a type.

Falabella

At a maximum height of 34 in (86 cm) the Falabella is the smallest horse in the world. It is named after the Falabella family on whose ranch near Buenos Aires the breed has been developed.

The Falabella is known to be descended from a small Thoroughbred that was crossed with Shetland Ponies to produce exceptionally small horses, but beyond that its origins are unclear. The genes producing the small size are still dominant today. Crossed with any mare a Falabella will produce a foal much smaller than the mare, and over a few generations a pony's descendants will shrink down to Falabella size.

The Falabella is a miniature horse, not a pony, and needs to be looked after as carefully as a Thoroughbred. The downgrading in size has reduced its strength so that it is not capable of carrying a rider. However, it is popular as a harness pony, and is also widely kept as a pet.

KEY FACTS

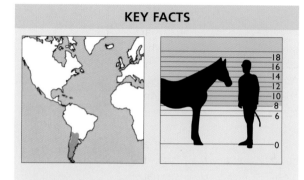

Color: All colors.
Height: Under seven hands.
Physique: Proportioned like a miniature horse; fine bones and small feet.
Character: Gentle and courageous.
Principal uses: Harness pony and pet.

Above: At under seven hands high, the Falabella is the smallest horse in the world. It was originally developed from a cross between a small Thoroughbred and a small Shetland. They are often kept as pets, and are sometimes driven in harness, but they are not suitable for riding.

ANCESTRY

Shetland Pony
Thoroughbred
Falabella

Criollo

The modern Criollo, the native horse of Argentina, has developed from Andalusians, Barbs, and Arabs brought over by the Spanish and which subsequently escaped. During the time that they ran wild on the Argentinian pampas plains, natural selection and adaptation to the rough conditions and extremes of temperature of this environment produced an exceptionally hardy breed.

The breed is quick, agile, and intelligent and made an excellent cattle horse, becoming the favourite mount of the Argentinian gauchos.

Attempts to improve the Criollo by crossing with other breeds have not been successful, and today the Argentinians follow a program of selective breeding. The best animals from which to breed are chosen by an annual ride of 470 miles (750 km), carrying 238 lb (108 kg) in weight, during which they may not be fed.

The Argentinian polo pony has been developed by crossing the Criollo with Thoroughbred stock, the Criollo providing stamina and toughness, and the Thoroughbred speed. Breeds such as the Crioulo in Brazil and the Llanero in Venezuela are also closely related to the Criollo, having developed in much the same way from similar Spanish stock. They now vary quite considerably from the basic Criollo type.

KEY FACTS

Color: Dun with dark points and dorsal stripe; sometimes roan, chestnut, bay.
Height: 14 hands.
Physique: Short, broad head, muscular neck, strong shoulders and broad chest, deep body, fine strong legs, small feet.
Character: Tough, willing, great endurance.
Principal uses: Riding and stock work.

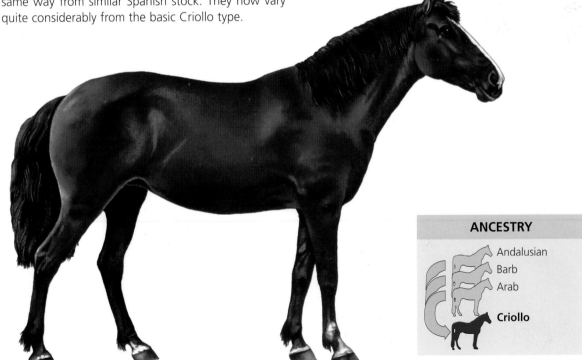

ANCESTRY

Andalusian
Barb
Arab
Criollo

Peruvian Paso

The Peruvian Paso is the best known of the South American Paso breeds that developed from the Andalusians, Barbs, and Spanish Jennets brought over by the Spanish Conquistadors.

The Peruvians needed a horse that could carry them comfortably for long distances over very rough and mountainous terrain, and they developed the breed carefully for over 300 years. The distinctive feature of the Peruvian Paso, as with the other Paso breeds, is its paso gait, which it is thought to have inherited from the Spanish Jennets. This is a lateral four-beat gait, in which the forelegs swing in an arc while the hindlegs take long, straight strides; the hindleg touches the ground fractionally ahead of the front leg. This produces a smooth, ambling pace that the horse can sustain for many miles at an average speed of about 11 mph (18 km/h).

The demands of working over long distances in the high Peruvian mountains gradually produced animals that were tough with great stamina. When breeding from them, the Peruvians looked for horses with a good paso gait, and also for those that were both proud and docile. This careful selection has produced a breed that is both tough and hardy, and exceptionally easy to break and handle. It is gaining popularity around the world due to its comfortable, easy gait and excellent temperament.

KEY FACTS

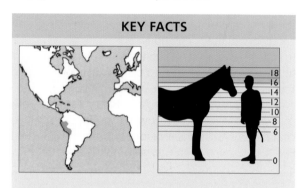

Color: Bay, chestnut, brown, black, gray.
Height: 14.2–15.2 hands.
Physique: Long crested neck, deep broad chest and body, strong fine legs, full mane and tail, high head carriage.
Character: Docile, great endurance.
Principal uses: Riding and stock work.

ANCESTRY

Andalusian

Barb

Spanish Jennet

Peruvian Paso Horse

Paso Fino

The Paso Fino of Puerto Rico is derived from the same origins as the Peruvian Paso.

It exhibits three paso gaits: the paso fino, performed at the pace of a slow walk; the paso carto, performed at the speed of a collected trot, at which it can cover very long distances; and the paso largo, performed at the speed of a slow canter.

Apart from the adaptations that the breed has made to the climate and conditions of South America, it is thought to be very similar to the original horses of the Spanish settlers.

In the United States, the American Paso Fino Horse Association is working toward merging the best characteristics from the various Paso breeds of Peru, Puerto Rico, Brazil, Venezuela and the Dominican Republic, to create an ideal Paso type.

KEY FACTS

Color: All colors.
Height: 14.3 hands.
Physique: Arab-type head, strong back and hindquarters, hard fine legs.
Character: Spirited, tractable.
Principal uses: Riding and stock work.

ANCESTRY

Andalusian
Barb
Spanish Jennet
Paso Fino

Galiceno

KEY FACTS

Color: Bay, black, dun, sorrel, gray.
Height: 12–13.2 hands.
Physique: Intelligent head, straight shoulders, narrow chest, short back, fine legs, small feet.
Character: Alert, kind, intelligent.
Principal uses: Ranch work, transport.

The Galiceno is descended from ponies of the Galicia region of Spain that were among those taken over to the New World by the Spanish Conquistadors. These were probably Garrano ponies, but might have included Minhos from northern Portugal as well. These horses accompanied the Spanish when they conquered Mexico, and it is there that the Galiceno breed developed, although more through natural selection than by selective breeding on the part of man.

Through the Garrano the Galiceno contains a fair amount of Arab blood, and shows many characteristics of the Arab. It is intelligent, tough, full of stamina, and has a kind, gentle temperament. It has the appearance of a small, narrow-framed horse, and has an unusual extra gait—a fast running walk—which makes it a comfortable ride over long distances. In its native Mexico it is used for ranch work and light transport work.

In 1959 Galicenos were first imported into the United States, and they have been very popular there. The Galiceno learns quickly and has proved to be very versatile. It is used there for ranch work and as a competition horse.

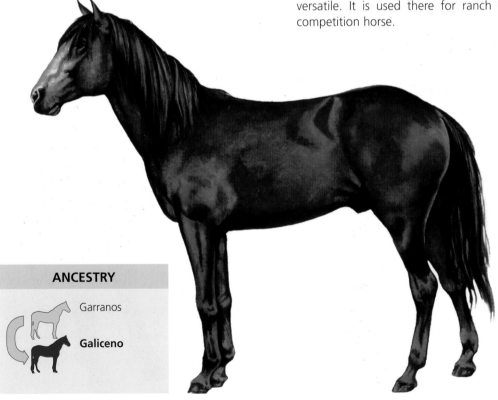

ANCESTRY

Garranos

Galiceno

Mangalarga

KEY FACTS

Color: Bay, chestnut, roan, gray.
Height: 15 hands.
Physique: Longish head, short back, powerful hindquarters, low-set tail, long legs.
Principal uses: Riding, stock work.

The Mangalarga breed of Brazil is about 100 years old, and is the result of crossing Crioulo mares with Andalusian and Altér Real stock.

This resulted in a fine riding horse which has a distinctive fifth gait between trot and canter, called the marcha, that produces a comfortable rocking movement.

The Campolino, also from Brazil, is a heavier version of the Mangalarga.

ANCESTRY

Crioulo
Andalusian
Altér Real

Mangalarga

Exmoor

The Exmoor is the oldest of all the British native breeds. It is thought to have existed in prehistoric times and was probably the pony that pulled the chariots of the Celts. The Exmoor area is quite isolated and the breed has remained remarkably pure. In fact, evidence suggests that the modern pony has changed little from its early ancestors.

The moorland environment is harsh and solitary, and in response the Exmoor has developed the toughness and resilience for which it is renowned. It can even endure winters that bring several feet of snow, without shelter or additional feed being provided. The Exmoor is also extremely strong; it can even carry adult farmers for a day's hunting or shepherding.

Exmoors still run wild in herds, but they are privately owned and registered in a stud book. The ponies are rounded up once a year and driven down to the farms for inspection. Those accepted as good specimens of the breed are branded and registered.

The Exmoor's qualities of hardiness and endurance have made it very popular as foundation breeding stock; it produces particularly good stock when crossed with Thoroughbreds. In recent years Exmoor ponies have been exported all over the world for this purpose.

Although ponies taken off the moor seem wild at first, they make excellent children's riding ponies if they are well trained.

KEY FACTS

Color: Bay, brown, or mouse dun; mealy muzzle; must not include white.
Height: Mares up to 12.2 hands; stallions and geldings up to 12.3 hands.
Physique: Broad forehead, thick neck, deep chest, short clean legs, hard feet.
Character: Intelligent, quick-witted, alert, kind.
Principal uses: Riding, foundation stock.

ANCESTRY

Celtic pony

Exmoor

Dartmoor

Dartmoors have roamed the desolate moorland of southern Devon for many centuries. They are closely related to the Exmoor and are probably descended from the same stock. They have developed the same qualities of hardiness and surefootedness in response to their environment.

The earliest record of the breed appears in the will of Bishop Aelwold of Crediton in 1012. It is known that during the tin-mining era on Dartmoor, the ponies were used to carry the tin down from the moors. Once the mines closed, however, they were left to roam free again.

For some time Dartmoors were crossed with other breeds, resulting in great variations in type. However, the formation of a breed society, and the setting down of entry requirements, at the end of the 19th century has gone a long way toward stabilizing the breed. Since that time, considerable progress has been made in producing a first-class children's riding pony; the breed is now also valued as foundation stock for larger all-round ponies.

The Dartmoor pony is reliable and sensible. It is also extremely versatile: it goes well over jumps, and can be used for hunting and in harness. Its high head carriage and broad shoulders make children who are learning to ride feel particularly safe on it, and this, coupled with its kind temperament and comfortable action, makes it an ideal first pony for children.

KEY FACTS

Color: Bay, brown, black.
Height: Up to 12.2 hands.
Physique: Small head, very small ears, strong neck, shoulders set well back, strong hindquarters, high-set full tail, slim, hard legs.
Character: Quiet, reliable, kind, sensible.
Principal uses: Excellent child's first pony.

ANCESTRY

Celtic pony

Dartmoor

Fell

The fell pony inhabits the uplands of Cumbria on the western side of the Pennine Hills. It is thought to be descended from the Celtic pony, but has also been influenced by the Friesian, and later by the Galloway pony. Friesian horses were brought over by the Frieslanders to help the Romans build Hadrian's Wall in AD120. When they had finished, they left behind a large group of Friesian stallions that bred with the native ponies to produce the Fell, and its neighbor, the Dales. Since that time the Fell has remained quite isolated, and today it breeds truer to type, and is more easily recognized, than any other native breed apart from the Exmoor.

The Fell is famous for its great strength. During the time that it was used for carrying lead from the local mines to the coast, it was reputed to have carried loads of 220 lb (100 kg) for 30 miles or more day after day. It was also used on the North Country farms for heavy agricultural work and harness work as well as shepherding and general riding. And on days off, the farmers would enter their ponies in local trotting races.

The modern Fell is extremely strong, and has plenty of stamina, making it suitable for harness work, for competitive events such as endurance riding, and for pleasure riding and trekking.

KEY FACTS

Color: Usually black; also brown, bay, gray; white markings on legs permitted.
Height: 13–14 hands.
Physique: Alert head, long neck, muscular body, strong legs with feathering, long and thick mane and tail.
Character: Hard-working, lively.
Principal uses: Riding, driving, trekking.

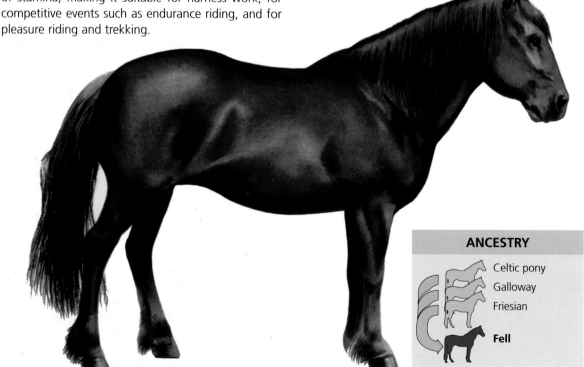

ANCESTRY

Celtic pony

Galloway

Friesian

Fell

Dales

ANCESTRY

Celtic pony
Friesian
Galloway
Welsh Cob

Dales

KEY FACTS

Color: Black or brown; white star permitted.
Height: 13.2–14.2 hands.
Physique: Neat head, strong neck, powerful compact body, short legs, thick mane and tail, feathering on feet.
Character: Sensible, quiet, hardworking.
Principal uses: Riding, agricultural work, trekking.

The Dales pony is closely related to the Fell, being descended from Celtic and Galloway pony origins. It inhabits the eastern side of the Pennine Hills.

Like the Fell, the Dales pony is immensely strong. It was widely used for transporting lead from the local mines to the coast ports and as a general packhorse. Since it could pull heavy loads, farmers found it extremely useful for all types of agricultural work. It also made a good riding horse, being surefooted and agile, and a fast trotter. In the 19th century, Dales mares were crossed with a Welsh cob called Comet, a champion in the local trotting races, in order to increase the overall speed of the breed, and all Dales can be traced back to this stallion.

With the advent of motorized transport, the breed's numbers declined markedly until in the 1950s it nearly became extinct. With the formation of the Dales Pony Society in 1963, however, both interest in the breed, and its numbers, have increased again.

It is an ideal pony for trekking; it is also good for general riding although, due to its strength, it is more suitable for an adult than a child.

Crossed with Thoroughbred blood, the Dales pony produces excellent jumpers and hunters.

New Forest

The origins of the New Forest pony are probably similar to those of the Exmoor and Dartmoor, as the forest it inhabited 1,000 years ago would have spread as far as Devon and Somerset. The earliest record of the breed occurred in the 11th century, during the rein of King Canute; horses were noted to be running wild in the forest.

The area is less remote than those inhabited by other native ponies, and over the centuries groups of other breeds were turned loose there, with the result that the New Forest pony now shows a range of types. Deliberate attempts were made to upgrade the wild ponies from time to time. In 1852, for example, Queen Victoria allowed an Arab stallion to run loose in the Forest for eight years to breed with the native mares. More recently, Thoroughbreds have also been used, as have stallions of other native breeds.

The New Forest is the second-largest of the native ponies. It has a narrower frame than the others, which makes it well suited as a children's pony, although it is strong enough to carry adults as well. Its quality as a riding and harness pony has made it popular all over the world.

New Forest ponies still run wild in the forest; the stallions being inspected for quality each year. The breed's long exposure to human visitors has caused it to lose much of its natural nervousness of people, and it is particularly tractable and docile.

KEY FACTS

Color: Any color except piebald or skewbald; white markings permitted.
Height: 12–14.2 hands.
Physique: Large head, long sloping shoulders, short back with deep girth, hard legs and good feet.
Character: Intelligent, willing, friendly, docile.
Principal uses: Children's riding pony.

ANCESTRY

Celtic pony
Native breeds
Thoroughbred
Arab

New Forest

Connemara

The Connemara is the only native pony breed of Ireland. It is an ancient breed, and has run free in the mountains of the west coast since prehistoric times.

Its origins are unclear, but it is thought to be descended from the same stock as the Highland, Shetland, Icelandic, and Norwegian Fjord ponies. However, the Connemara is lighter and more athletic than the other native breeds, and has a pretty, almost Oriental look. One theory put forward to explain this is that the breed was crossed with Spanish Jennets shipwrecked with the Spanish Armada in 1588. It is also possible that Galway merchants trading with Spain in the 16th and 17th centuries imported some Spanish and Oriental horses, which subsequently escaped and bred with the wild native ponies.

Until recently the Connemara was used as a general-purpose animal. However, today it is principally valued as a children's riding pony. It has a free, fluent action. and can perform in all areas of equitation from dressage to hunting. However, it has a particular talent for jumping; and crossed with Thoroughbred stock it has produced some highly successful competition horses. It has also undoubtedly contributed to the development of the Irish Half-bred.

KEY FACTS

Color: Usually gray; can be black, brown, bay.
Height: 13–14 hands.
Physique: Intelligent, well carried head, medium-length neck on sloping shoulders, deep compact body, short legs.
Character: Intelligent, kind, sensible, tractable.
Principal uses: Riding, jumping, driving.

ANCESTRY

Celtic pony
Spanish Jennet
Arab
Thoroughbred

Connemara

Shetland

KEY FACTS

Color: Black, bay, brown, chestnut, gray, part-colors.

Height: Up to 10.2 hands.

Physique: Small head, sloping shoulders, deep thick-set body, short back, short legs with some feathering, small open feet.

Character: Independent, headstrong.

Principal uses: Riding and harness pony, pet.

The Shetland pony comes from the Shetland Islands off northern Scotland, where it was isolated for nearly 2,000 years before being brought over to the mainland during the 19th century. The origins of the breed are not known, but it is thought to be descended from a "dwarf" Exmoor type.

During the centuries of isolation on the islands the breed remained completely pure. In the 19th century, however, its value as a pit pony was recognized, and many were taken from the Shetlands and put to work down the mines. As a result, it was bred for quantity rather than quality, and the breed deteriorated until the late 19th century, when breeding farms were created to re-establish a good Shetland type. It became the first native pony to have its own society, and the stud book was opened in 1890.

At a maximum height of 10.2 hands the Shetland is the smallest of the native breeds, yet relative to its size it is the strongest pony in the world. Until quite recently it provided the only form of transport on its native islands, pulling carts of peat (for fuel) and seaweed (for fertilizer).

Although its size makes it an ideal pony for small children, its headstrong and independent character demands firm, though kind, handling to keep it under control. However, it makes an excellent harness-pony, and its performances in harness are the highlight of many shows.

ANCESTRY

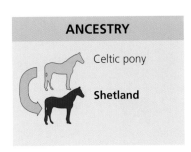

Celtic pony

Shetland

Highland

The Highland pony of northern Scotland is probably descended from the same Celtic type as the Exmoor, and has subsequently been influenced by the now-extinct Galloway, and later by Arab blood.

It was originally divided into two strains which developed separately according to local conditions and requirements. The mainland strain, known as the Garron, was the larger of the two, and at 14.2 hands is the largest and strongest of the native breeds. The Western Isles strain averaged about 12.2 hands. However, cross-breeding has now more or less eliminated these distinctions.

The Highland pony was the traditional partner of the Scottish crofters, who used it as a general-purpose working pony. They were able to carry great weights, while working on the craggy and difficult terrain of the Scottish Highlands produced remarkable agility and surefootedness, creating the ideal pack-horse for the mountains. However, they are not built for speed; the walk and trot being their two natural gaits.

The Highland pony is still found mainly in Scotland, where it is used in many roles. The larger ones are used by deer-stalkers to bring the carcasses down from the mountains; they make good trekking ponies, and are used for tree-felling work and shepherding. The smaller ones make good children's riding ponies.

KEY FACTS

Color: Dun, ranging from golden-blue to silver-blue with dorsal stripe; sometimes black, gray-black, or brown.
Height: 13–14.2 hands.
Physique: Neat head, solid deep body, short strong legs, well-shaped hard hooves.
Character: Docile, intelligent, sensitive, trusting.
Principal uses: Riding and trekking.

ANCESTRY

Celtic pony
Galloway
Arab
Clydesdale

Highland Garron

87

Welsh Ponies

The Welsh native ponies are considered by many to be the prettiest of the British pony breeds. The Welsh Pony stud book is divided into four sections: A, B, C, and D.

SECTION A

The Welsh Mountain Pony (section A) is the original, and smallest, of the Welsh breeds, and is probably descended from the Celtic pony. There are references to wild mountain ponies going as far back as Roman times, and Julius Caesar established a stud at Lake Bala, Merionethshire. Within the last two to three hundred years, two Arab stallions have been allowed to roam the Welsh Mountains to improve the native stock, and this probably accounts for the breed's Arab looks.

Because it has lived on the mountains for over 1,000 years, this breed has become tough, resilient, surefooted, and quick. In addition, it combines all the best pony qualities—courage, endurance, intelligence, and gentleness. It also has natural jumping ability. As a result, it makes an excellent children's pony, and many children's riding ponies today have some Welsh blood in them. In addition, it has a good trot and goes well in harness.

KEY FACTS

Color: Any color except piebald or skewbald.
Height: Not over 12 hands.
Physique: Small head, concave face, crested neck, sloping shoulders, short back, tail set high, short legs, neat feet.
Character: Intelligent, kind, brave, spirited.
Principal uses: Riding, foundation stock for riding ponies.

The Welsh Mountain Pony has always bred out in the mountains, ensuring the continuation of the breed's natural qualities, and breeders from around the world import fresh stock from Wales to replenish and improve their own breeding stock. The Welsh Mountain has been used as foundation stock for three other Welsh breeds.

ANCESTRY

Celtic pony
Arab

Welsh

Section A

SECTION B

The Welsh Pony (section B) has been bred as a quality children's riding pony. It was created by crossing Welsh Mountain mares with a small Thoroughbred stallion called Merlin, a direct descendant of the Darley Arabian (see page 59), and these ponies are also known as Merlins. Arab and section C blood may also have been added. It is similar to the Welsh Mountain except that it is taller and more lightly built. It has retained all the pony characteristics.

SECTION C

The Welsh Pony (section C) is a smaller version of the Welsh Cob. It is energetic and brave, and very versatile. At one time it was used mainly in harness, although there is not much demand for it in that role now. However, it is ideally suited to the popular pastime of trekking as it can carry an adult comfortably. It is also a good hunting pony for a child.

SECTION D

The Welsh Cob (section D) is a larger version of the cob-type pony. It is thought to have been created

KEY FACTS

Color: As for Welsh Mountain.
Size: Not over 13.2 hands.
Physique: As for Welsh Mountain; look for action, temperament, and looks of quality riding pony.
Character: As for Welsh Mountain.

around the 12th century, by crossing Welsh Mountain ponies with Spanish horses. It may also be related to the now extinct Old Welsh Cart-horse. During medieval times it was used as a pack-horse and for riding. Welsh Cobs are good trotters, and the breed has been used to create and improve trotting breeds around the world.

Section B

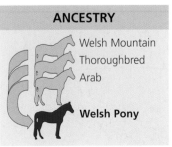

ANCESTRY

Welsh Mountain
Thoroughbred
Arab

Welsh Pony

Cleveland Bay

The Cleveland Bay is probably the oldest of the British horse breeds. Its origins are thought to go back to a type of horse brought to Britain by the Romans. Certainly by medieval times, a type of pack-horse called the Chapman Horse was being used by travelling merchants, or "chapmen," in the north of England. It is from this horse that the Cleveland is descended.

The breed was developed in north-east England, where it was used as an all-rounder, for agricultural and draft work, in harness, and for riding and hunting. However, it was as a pack animal that the Cleveland was most valued, its strength and endurance enabling it to carry very heavy loads.

During the 19th century, owing to its strength, good looks, and tractable nature, it became popular as a carriage-horse. At this time the breed received an injection of Thoroughbred blood, and the result was so popular that another breed with additional Thoroughbred blood, the Yorkshire Coach Horse, was created. This classy and fashionable carriage horse became extinct in the 1930s.

It is as a carriage-horse that the Cleveland Bay excels today, and it is consistently successful in driving competitions. It also has natural jumping ability, and crossed with the Thoroughbred, produces international-class jumpers and dressage horses.

KEY FACTS

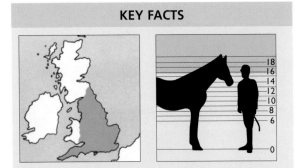

Color: Bay; a small star is allowed.
Height: 15.2–16 hands.
Physique: Large head, long neck, long deep-girthed body, short strong clean legs.
Character: Intelligent, sensible, calm, tractable.
Principal uses: Driving, riding.

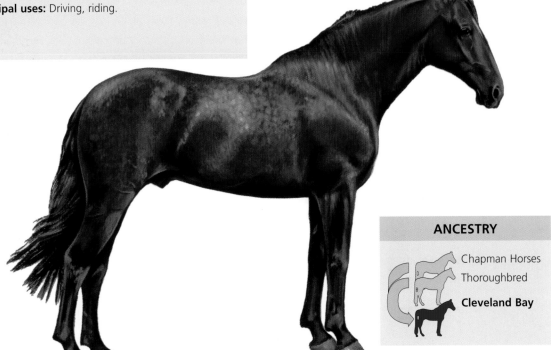

ANCESTRY

Chapman Horses
Thoroughbred
Cleveland Bay

Hackney

The development of the modern Hackney is well documented.

The Hackney Horse was created from the British regional breeds of trotters, the Norfolk and Yorkshire Trotters, which had been developed as fast-trotting harness horses. In the early 19th century, these two breeds were crossed to produce the lighter Hackney Horse. At this time proper roads were being built, and the Hackney, with its elegant, fast-trotting gait and powers of endurance, provided a quick means of transport.

In the middle of the 19th century the Hackney Pony was created by crossing the Hackney Horse with Fell mares. The Hackney blood provided speed and elegance; the Fell power and a high knee action. The Hackney Pony should look like a pony type, with a small, intelligent head, but it shares the features of spectacular action, high spirits, and endurance with the Horse.

The special characteristic of the Hackneys is their action. At the trot they have a high, ground-covering knee action, the foreleg being raised up and thrown forward in an extravagant movement. They are a regular feature item in the showring, as well as being popular in competition classes.

KEY FACTS

Color: Bay, dark brown, black.
Height: 14–15.3 hands (Horse); under 14 hands (Pony).
Physique: Small head with convex face, long neck, compact body with deep chest, short legs with strong hocks, tail set and carried high, fine silky coat.
Character: Spirited, alert, courageous.
Principal use: Driving.

ANCESTRY

Norfolk Roadster
Thoroughbred

Hackney Horse

Shire

The Shire is the greatest of the heavy horse breeds, standing at up to 18 hands high, and weighing over a ton (approximately 1,000 kg).

The breed is probably descended from the Great Horses and Old English Blacks that were ridden into battle by the medieval knights. The ancestry of these breeds is uncertain but probably stems in part from the Friesian and Flanders horses of northern Europe.

The Old English Black was a popular draft horse, especially in the Midland counties of England, in the 18th and 19th centuries. It was particularly in demand for transporting the raw materials and products of the Industrial Revolution.

During the mid nineteenth century, indiscriminate breeding to fill the demand for draft horses led to a deterioration in the quality of the breed, and in 1878 the Shire Horse Society (at first known as the Cart Horse Society) was formed in order to raise and maintain standards again.

These marvellous, aristocratic horses are a pleasure to work with. Their popularity, and ability to draw large crowds at shows, has ensured the breed's survival despite the fact that it is no longer in demand as a working horse.

ANCESTRY

Friesian
Old English
Black Horse
Flanders Horse
Native stock

Shire

KEY FACTS

Color: Black, bay, gray, with white markings.
Height: 16.2–17 hands; stallions can reach 18 hands.
Physique: Slightly convex profile, wide chest, deep broad girth, dense muscular body, long legs with feathering.
Character: Docile, gentle, kind, hard-working.
Principal uses: Draft, showing.

Suffolk Punch

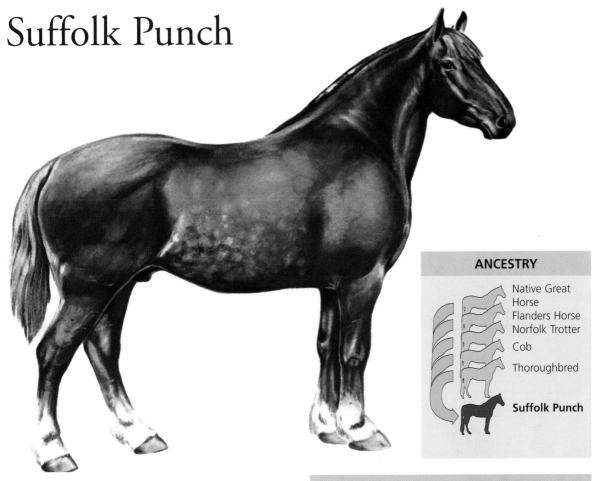

ANCESTRY

Native Great Horse
Flanders Horse
Norfolk Trotter
Cob
Thoroughbred

Suffolk Punch

KEY FACTS

Color: Chestnut, in seven shades—red, gold, copper, yellow, liver, light, dark.
Height: 16 hands.
Physique: Large head, deep neck, massive shoulders, round compact body, clean legs, short cannon bone.
Character: Gentle, active, docile.
Principal uses: Draft, showing.

The Suffolk Punch is the purest bred of the British heavy horses. All members of the breed can be traced to a trotting horse foaled in 1760, although the breed was mentioned in records as early as 1506.

It may be descended from the Great Horse, and in the 16th and 17th centuries Flanders stallions are known to have been put to Suffolk mares. In the 18th century attempts were made to introduce a smarter element into the breed by crossing it with Norfolk Trotter, Cob, and even Thoroughbred blood.

The Suffolk Punch has many assets. It is very long-lived, often working well into its twenties, and living beyond the age of 30. It can thrive on poor keep. Its large, broad shoulders and short legs give it tremendous pulling power. And it always breeds true to color—chestnut.

In earlier times the Suffolk was considered the best horse for agricultural work. Today, its personality and presence ensure that it is preserved for its own sake.

Irish Draft

ANCESTRY

Native stock
Connemara
Thoroughbred

Irish Draught

The Irish Draft was created in the 18th century by crossing Thoroughbred stallions with native Irish mares. Its previous origins are unknown.

This cross-breeding resulted in a fine, powerful, and versatile horse. It was strong enough for heavy agricultural work and carriage-driving. At the same time, it was an active horse with powerful hindquarters, making it excellent for riding and hunting. The Irish Draft flourished until the agricultural recession in 1879. After that its numbers declined sharply until the Irish Government stepped in, in 1907, to help promote the interests of the breed. It was found that when crossed with the Thoroughbred, it produced excellent hunting and competition horses that were popular all over the world, and Ireland became a major exporter of these horses.

Today the number of purebred horses has declined badly, but the Irish Government is again taking action to restore the breed. There is also an effective Irish Draft Horse society working to preserve it.

KEY FACTS

Color: Bay, brown, chestnut, gray.
Height: 15–17 hands.
Physique: Intelligent head, short muscular neck, long powerful body, strong legs, very little feather.
Character: Quiet, alert, sensible, willing.
Principal uses: Hunting, cross-breeding for competition horses.

Irish Half-bred

KEY FACTS

Color: Any solid color.
Height: 16.1 hands.
Physique: Varies; classic hunting or showjumping type.
Character: Intelligent, bold, sensible.
Principal uses: Hunting, showjumping, eventing.

The Irish Half-bred, or Irish Hunter, was until recently classed as a type, and the breed is still being developed. It is produced by crossing a Thoroughbred with an Irish Draft. This has produced top-class competitive horses that are outstanding as showjumpers and eventers.

Since the 1970s the Irish Horse Board has been overseeing the development of the breed. It still shows a variety of types, depending on the parentage, but the majority have good, alert heads and are strongly built.

Below: The Irish Half-bred has produced many top-class show jumpers, such as Ryan's Son, seen here in action at Rotterdam.

ANCESTRY

Irish Draft
Thoroughbred
Connemara

Irish Half-bred

95

Anglo-Arab

Although the Anglo-Arab, which is a cross between an Arab and a Thoroughbred, is found in many parts of the world, in France it has been developed as a distinct breed.

The French Anglo-Arab originated from English Thoroughbreds and purebred Arabs during the 1840s. In the beginning there were two strains: the southern part-bred and the purebred. The southern part-bred was developed in the Limousin area of south-west France by crossing Arabs or Thoroughbreds with native mares that were themselves of Arab or Oriental origins. The purebred Anglo Arab was developed from direct crosses between Arab and Thoroughbred blood. Because the part-bred and purebred strains are now very similar in temperament and type, they have been combined in one stud book which is open to any horse resulting from a combination of English Thoroughbred, purebred Arab, and Anglo-Arab as long as it has at least 25 percent Arab blood.

The Anglo-Arab has excelled as a competition horse, and Anglo-Arab stallions have been used to upgrade the quality of other breeds, particularly the Selle Francaise, or French Riding Horse. This term covers the breed previously known as the Anglo Norman, created by crossing local Normandy mares with Thoroughbred blood, together with other French pedigree riding horses.

KEY FACTS

Color: Most solid colors.
Height: 16 hands.
Physique: Delicate head, withers set well back, deep chest, short back, well-proportioned hindquarters, tail set high, long slender legs.
Character: Brave, spirited, intelligent.
Principal uses: Riding and competition.

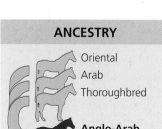
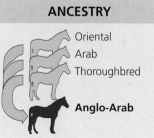

ANCESTRY

Oriental
Arab
Thoroughbred

Anglo-Arab

French Trotter

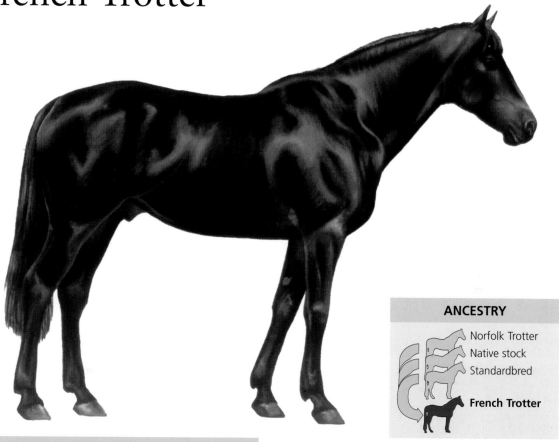

ANCESTRY

Norfolk Trotter
Native stock
Standardbred
French Trotter

KEY FACTS

Color: Chestnut, bay; brown most common.
Height: 16.1 hands.
Physique: Alert head, strong straight shoulders, short back, well-muscled powerful hindquarters, long hard legs with short cannon bone.
Character: Willing, tough.
Principal uses: Harness-racing, general riding, cross breeding.

The French Trotter was developed principally in Normandy during the middle part of the 19th century. The first trotting course to open in France was at Cherbourg in 1836, and others sprang up soon afterward. As the sport grew in popularity, so did the demand for good horses.

The early horses were produced by crossing good English trotting blood, usually Norfolk Trotters, with the Anglo-Norman to produce a strain of Anglo-Norman specially suited to the sport.

Later in the century these Anglo-Normans were further improved by the importation of foreign stallions, notably the Standardbred from America, which by that time had been developed into a very fast harness-horse.

In 1922 a stud book was opened for Anglo Normans that had proved themselves by trotting one kilometer in 1 minute 42 seconds in a race. These horses came to be known as French Trotters, and the new breed was established.

Camargue

These famous horses, which have captured the imagination of horse-lovers all over the world, have roamed wild in the marshlands of the Camargue region, in the Rhône Delta of France, for many hundreds of years. Their origins are unknown but it is possible that they can be traced back to horses known to have lived in the area in prehistoric times. From their appearance it is very likely that they are in part descended from Arab and Barb horses brought to the area by the Romans and later the Moors.

The Camargue live on rough marsh grass and saltwater. In response to the climate and environment of the marshlands, they have developed into rugged, robust, surefooted horses.

The Camargue has a high-stepping walk, a fast gallop, and can twist and turn quickly. Although essentially wild, those that are caught and broken make good riding horses. They are popular with the *gardiens* (Camargue cowboys) for herding cattle, and

Above: The Camargue is fast, agile, and quick-witted. It is the favorite mount of the *gardiens*, who use them for herding cattle, and in particular for rounding up the black bulls of the area.

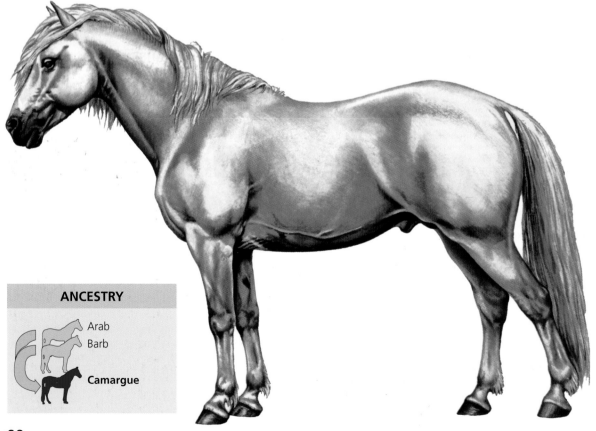

ANCESTRY

Arab
Barb

Camargue

especially for rounding up the equally famous black bulls of the Camargue that are bred for bullfighting. They are also used for pony-trekking in the Camargue area.

The Camargue has been officially recognized as a breed since 1968. There are about 30 herds in existence at the moment. Although the horses run wild and their breeding is not controlled, round-ups take place once a year and young stallions at about the age of three that are not of sufficient quality to be allowed to breed are removed and gelded. This has led to a notable improvement in the breed. The foals are born dark, and turn the characteristic gray color as they mature. They grow whiter as they age.

Above: The Camargue is known as the White Horse of the Sea. It is an ancient breed, and its appearance suggests that it has Arab ancestry. It still runs wild in the marshlands of the Rhone Delta, and has only recently been recognized as a breed.

KEY FACTS

Color: Gray.
Height: 13.2–14.2 hands.
Physique: Large Oriental-type head with straight profile, short shoulders and back, slight hindquarters, fine legs, large feet.
Character: Tractable when tamed.
Principal uses: Herding and trekking; also roams wild.

Percheron

KEY FACTS

Color: Gray or black.

Height: 15.2–17 hands.

Physique: Straight profile, deep crested neck, deep powerful chest, short body, very powerful hindquarters, thick muscular legs, as little feathering as possible.

Character: Active, intelligent, good-natured.

Principal uses: Draft.

The Percheron is the most famous and most numerous of the French draft horses, both in France and around the world. Its intelligent and docile nature inspire great enthusiasm and loyalty in its admirers, and much attention is paid to the quality and purity of the breed.

The breed originated in north-west France, in the Paris-basin area of La Perche, probably through the mixing of local Norman horses with Arabs and other Oriental breeds left behind in western Europe by the Moors. This produced a heavy horse that was used at first by the medieval knights. Subsequently the breed was crossed with heavier draft breeds to produce a very strong working horse. It is still used for agricultural work today, and is also popular in the showring.

An infusion of Arab blood in the 19th century contributed to the Percheron being active and lively. It also has great elegance for a heavy breed.

There is a smaller type of Percheron, known as the Postier Percheron.

The Boulonnais, another heavy draft breed from northern France, is descended in part from the same Oriental stock, together with Andalusian blood, and is very similar to the Percheron.

ANCESTRY

Oriental
Heavy draft breeds
Norman

Percheron

Draft Breton

KEY FACTS

Color: Gray, chestnut, bay.
Height: 15–16 hands; Postier Breton not above 15 hands.
Physique: Wide short head, strong neck, broad body, short muscular legs, a little feathering; Postier Breton lighter and more elegant.
Character: Lively, intelligent, good-natured.
Principal uses: Agricultural work, light draft.

There are two types of Breton: the Draft Breton and the Postier Breton, both of which were developed in the Brittany area of north-west France.

The Draft Breton developed originally from the Roussin, a native of Brittany in the Middle Ages. The Roussin was a riding horse known for its comfortable, ambling, fourth gait. When a heavier horse was needed for draft and agricultural work, the Roussin was crossed with the Percheron, the Ardennes (an ancient, gentle and particularly tough breed of draft horse from the Ardennes region of France and Belgium), and the Boulonnais (an active and lively draft breed from northern France), giving rise to the Draft Breton.

During the 19th century the Draft Breton was crossed with Norfolk Trotter and Hackney blood, creating the Postier Breton, a lighter, more elegant horse with a smart action that was used as a coach and light draft horse.

The Breton is still used today for agricultural work in Brittany, in the Midi vineyards, and in some of the third-world countries.

Today the two types of Breton have their own divisions within one stud book.

ANCESTRY

Native stock
Percheron
Ardennes
Boulonnais

Draft Breton

Friesian

The Friesian is one of the oldest European horse breeds. Its origins are unknown, but a type of heavy horse is known to have existed in the Friesland region of the northern Netherlands over 3,000 years ago. The Friesian was popular with the Romans, who took it over to Britain where it contributed toward the development of the Fell and Dales ponies. It was popular with the knights of medieval times, and it appears in paintings by many of the Dutch Old Masters. By this time it had probably been crossed with the Andalusian, Arab, and Barb.

The Friesian's outstanding feature is its very fast trot with a high knee-action. During the 19th century, it was used to improve other trotting breeds, such as the Orlov Trotter and the Norfolk Trotter (through which it influenced the Morgan).

The Friesian's popularity for cross-breeding, coupled with the decline in demand for working horses, caused its numbers to drop drastically before World War I, when action was taken to save the breed with the help of Oldenburg stallions (a breed originally derived from the Friesian).

The Friesian is easy to train, and has a spectacular action, making it successful as a competition and show carriage-horse, and in the circus-ring.

The Friesian was crossed with the Oldenburg and East Friesian to produce the Groningen, a slightly larger horse that is used for driving, riding and light draft-work.

KEY FACTS

Color: Black only.
Height: 15 hands.
Physique: Fine long head, crested neck, strong compact body, rounded hindquarters, short legs with feathering, very full mane and tail.
Character: Quiet, willing, sensitive, hard-working, active.
Principal uses: Driving.

Belgian Heavy Draft

ANCESTRY

Flanders Horse

Belgian Heavy Draft

The Belgian Heavy Draft (also known as the Brabant), from the Brabant region of Belgium, has a very ancient lineage. It is thought to be a direct descendant of the Flanders Horse, one of the medieval warhorses in northern Europe.

Following the Reformation, other bloodlines were introduced in an attempt to change the Brabant, but they were not very successful, and ever since that time breeders have worked only with pure Brabant strains. The result is a magnificent horse that always breeds true to type.

It is one of the strongest of the heavy breeds, and has always worked as an all-round agricultural horse in Belgium. Its great strength and good nature have made it very popular, and it has been exported all over the world, especially to America. It has been used to found breeds of heavy horse, such as the Rhineland from Germany, and to improve other breeds of heavy horse, such as the Ardennes, whose size it has increased.

KEY FACTS

Color: Most are red roan with black points; sometimes bay, brown, dun, gray.

Height: 16.2–17 hands.

Physique: Relatively small square head, strong deep neck, powerful shoulders, short compact body, powerful hindquarters, short strong legs with some feathering.

Character: Docile, willing, active, bold.

Principal uses: Draft.

Franches Montagnes

The Franches Montagnes (also known as the Freiburger) is a light draft horse from the Jura Mountains of Switzerland. Its origins are a mixture of Norman, Anglo-Norman, Thoroughbred, and draft breeds.

Having developed in the mountains, the Franches Montagnes is agile, strong, surefooted, and full of stamina. It has been an invaluable working horse for the Swiss farmers, who have used it for all types of agricultural work until quite recently, and still use it on the higher fields that are too steep for a tractor. Its value is also recognized by the Swiss Army, who depend on it for transporting men and equipment quickly through the mountains.

Because of its importance to Swiss agriculture and defense, and because it is also seen as a good source of alternative energy and transport by the Swiss, the government controls the breeding program at the state-financed National Stud at Avenches. Because it is bred for character and ability rather than conformation, there is no fixed type.

The Franches Montagnes has also been used to develop a new breed, the Freiburger Saddle-horse, by crossing it with the Shagya Arab. The Freiburger Saddle-horse has an excellent temperament.

KEY FACTS

Color: Most solid colors.
Height: 14.3–15.2 hands.
Physique: Conformation varies; small head, compact body, strong legs, a little feathering.
Character: Docile, energetic.
Principal uses: Agricultural and army work.

ANCESTRY

Norman
Anglo-Norman
Thoroughbred
Draft breeds

Franches Montagnes

Trakehner

The Trakehner originally came from the area once known as East Prussia, now part of Poland. The breed was originally developed at the Trakehnen stud, which was established in 1732. The local Schwieken horses were used as foundation stock, and crossed with Thoroughbred and Arab blood to produce an elegant coach and cavalry horse.

The breed was badly depleted during World War II, and in the winter of 1945 about 700 Trakehner mares and a few stallions travelled west with refugees fleeing from the Russians. These horses were used to re-establish the breed in Germany. It has been carefully nurtured since that time, and today is one of the most elegant of horses. It also breeds very true to type.

The Trakehner's good looks, free, extravagant action, and versatility have made it popular as a show and dressage horse as well as for general riding.

The Trakehners that were left behind in Poland have been used to create the Wiekopolski breed. It was one of several breeds used to create the Wurttemburg, a good heavyweight riding and light draft horse. It has also been used to refine other breeds, such as the Hanoverian.

KEY FACTS

Color: Any solid color, usually dark.
Height: 16–16.2 hands.
Physique: Elegant head, long neck, prominent withers, deep chest, strong medium-length back, rounded hindquarters, slender legs and good feet.
Character: Tractable, spirited, courageous, versatile.
Principal uses: General riding, competition.

ANCESTRY

Schwieken
Arab
Thoroughbred

Trakehner

Hanoverian

Many of the German breeds are defined according to the area that they come from, and the Hanoverian originates from Hanover in north-western Germany. Since it was created in the early 18th century, it has been altered quite considerably in order to adapt it for different uses at different times.

The breed was founded in 1735 by Royal Decree at the Celle State Stud. Holstein stallions were used to lighten the native mares descended from the Great War-horse of the Middle Ages, to produce horses that were good for agricultural and coaching work. This process was continued by crossing with Thoroughbreds and Cleveland Bays imported from England and, toward the end of the 18th century, other imported breeds such as Andalusians.

In 1867 a breed society was formed with the aim of producing a horse equally suited to coach and military work, and remarkable results were achieved. However, after World War I, horses were no longer needed in the same numbers by the military, and the breed society re-stated its aims: to produce a bold horse good for general farm, coach, and riding work. From that time all stallions have been tested for speed, strength, and endurance before being allowed to breed.

After World War II, the Hanoverian was no longer needed for farm work or coach work, and the society again re-stated its aims: to produce a riding horse of "superior performance." Thoroughbred, Trakehner, and Arab blood has been used to refine the Hanoverian into a top-class, athletic, strong, and good-tempered riding and competition horse.

Hanoverians have excelled in showjumping, eventing, and dressage competitions at international level, and the breed is now also widely used to upgrade the quality of other sports horses around the world.

ANCESTRY

Great War-horse
Holstein
Thoroughbred
Cleveland Bay
Andalusian
Trakehner
Arab

Hanoverian

The Hanoverian has also been used in the creation of new breeds. It has been crossed with Arab and Thoroughbred blood to produce the Westphalian, an excellent riding horse that is nearly as numerous in Germany as the Hanoverian.

The Hanoverian, together with Thoroughbred and Trakehner blood, has created another excellent, athletic riding horse, the Danish Sport Horse, which is particularly successful in dressage competitions.

The Hanoverian is closely related to the Mecklenburg of East Germany, as similar bloodlines were used to create both breeds, and much cross-breeding has taken place between them. The Mecklenburg is the slightly smaller of the two, and is now bred as an all-round riding horse.

Below: Dynasty, ridden by Cynthia Ishoy, competing for Canada at the Olympic Games in 1988. This horse demonstrates the style, athleticism, and supreme elegance characteristic of the Hanoverian.

KEY FACTS

Color: All solid colors.
Height: 15.3–17 hands.
Physique: Varies; compact, powerful body, short strong legs.
Character: Intelligent, sensible, willing, bold.
Principal uses: Competition and general riding.

Oldenburg

The Oldenburg has flourished in the north-west region of Germany since the 17th century.

The breed was based on the Friesian horses of the Netherlands. In the beginning, these heavy draft horses were crossed with Andalusians and Barbs to produce a lighter type of working horse, which was refined still further during the 19th century by crossing with Cleveland Bays, Thoroughbreds, Anglo-Normans, and Hanoverians.

At this time, the breed was used as a high-class coach horse. It was also used for agricultural work and by the military. After World War I, it was no longer needed by the army, but continued to be in demand as a farm horse and coach horse until World War II. When it was no longer needed as a working horse, breeders began to cross it with Thoroughbred and Trakehner blood, in order to refine and lighten the breed to make it suitable for all-round riding.

The Oldenburg, together with the Thoroughbred, Cleveland Bay, and Norman, has been used to modify the old Rotteler draft breed to produce a riding horse that is now known as the Bavarian Warm-blood.

0KEY FACTS

Color: Any solid color; black, brown or bay most common.
Height: 16.2–17.2 hands.
Physique: Plain head, straight profile, strong neck, muscular chest and body, strong hindquarters, short legs.
Character: Bold, sensible.
Principal uses: Riding, competition, driving.

ANCESTRY

Friesian
Andalusian
Barb
Hanoverian
Cleveland Bay
Thoroughbred
Anglo-Norman

Oldenburg

East Friesian

The East Friesian is from the East Friesland region of Germany. The breed was developed from the Oldenburg, its close neighbor, and until World War II the two breeds were constantly exchanged and inter-bred.

However, since World War II the two breeds have been separated and have developed differently.

Cross-breeding with Arab and Hanoverian blood has refined and lightened the East Friesian, added strength and compactness, and given it a distinctive head. It has an excellent temperament, and is used as an all-round riding, competition, and harness horse.

KEY FACTS

Color: Any solid color.
Height: 15.2–16.2 hands.
Physique: Similar to the Oldenburg but lighter, and with a more elegant head.
Character: Bold, spirited, good-natured.
Principal uses: General riding, driving.

ANCESTRY

Oldenburg
Arab
Hanoverian

East Friesian

Holstein

The Holstein is probably the oldest of the German horse breeds. It comes from the marshlands of Schleswig-Holstein in northern Germany, and is known to have been bred there since the 14th century. In the beginning, Andalusians and Neapolitans were crossed with the local Marsh Horse (one of the Great Horse types) to produce a large, powerful horse that was popular all over Europe.

During the 19th century, the Holstein was crossed with Cleveland Bays and Thoroughbreds to refine the breed and produce a powerful carriage-horse with a high-stepping action and great stamina. The Cleveland Bay and Thoroughbred blood also contributed to the breed's jumping ability and talent for dressage.

The breed's numbers had dwindled by the end of World War II, and since that time great success has been achieved in building up and further refining the breed using Thoroughbred blood to produce top-quality competition horses.

Today the Holstein is successful in all areas of competitive riding at the highest level.

The Holstein is one of several breeds that have contributed to the Swiss Half-bred. This outstanding horse is powerful and athletic, and has a good temperament. It has been successful at the highest level.

KEY FACTS

Color: Most solid colors.
Height: 16–17 hands.
Physique: Elegant head, strong neck, powerful shoulders, deep girth, compact body, strong hindquarters, short legs.
Character: Intelligent, willing, bold, versatile, good-natured.
Principal uses: General riding, competition.

ANCESTRY

Marsh Horse
Andalusian
Neapolitan
Cleveland Bay
Thoroughbred

Holstein

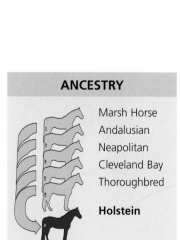

Schleswig Heavy Draft

The Schleswig was developed in the Schleswig Holstein region of Germany during the 19th century to meet the heavy demand for horses for agricultural and draft work.

There were two major influences on the development of the breed: the Jutland, its neighbor in Denmark, which is thought to have been ridden by the Vikings and which was certainly used as a warhorse by the Danes; and the Suffolk Punch from England. Other breeds, such as the Breton, Boulonnais (an elegant, active heavy draft horse from northern France), Cleveland Bay, and Thoroughbred, have subsequently been used to correct faults in the breed, and have also had the effect of making it lighter and more lively.

It was used as an all-round heavy draft horse for industrial and agricultural work and by the army for moving artillery.

KEY FACTS

Color: Usually chestnut with flaxen mane and tail.
Height: 15.1–16 hands.
Physique: Large head with convex profile, short powerful neck, deep girth, long flat body, short muscular legs with a little feathering.
Character: Willing, kind.
Principal uses: Draft.

ANCESTRY

Ancient stock
Jutland Suffolk Punch
Boulonnais
Breton

Schleswig

Lipizzaner

The Lipizzaner is Austria's most celebrated horse, known the world over for its displays of high-school dressage with the Spanish Riding School of Vienna.

The Lipizzaner was first bred at Lipizza stud (now in Yugoslavia) by Archduke Charles of Austria. High-school equitation was fashionable in the courts of Europe at the time and he wanted horses that would excel at it. In 1580 he imported Andalusian stallions, which were considered best for high school equitation, and crossed them with local mares.

Over the next 300 years, other breeds were also imported and crossed with the stock—notably the Neapolitan (an Italian breed, now extinct, produced by crossing Andalusians with Arab and Barb blood), Kladrubers, and Fredericksborgs (both also of Andalusian descent). All Lipizzaners can be traced back to six stallions from this time: Pluto (Fredericksborg), Conversano and Neapolitano (Neapolitan), Favory and Maestoso (Kladruber), and Siglavy (Arab).

Later attempts at crossing with other blood, such as Thoroughbred and Anglo-Arab, were not very successful, and the Andalusian has always remained the most important line.

When the Austro-Hungarian stud was broken up in 1918, the Lipizza stud was relocated in Italy, and the quality of the horses there was allowed to deteriorate. However, after World War II, Lipizza became part of Yugoslavia, new stock was imported, and the breed is now flourishing there again.

THE SPANISH RIDING SCHOOL

The Spanish Riding School of Vienna was originally founded in 1758 to educate the nobility in the art of horsemanship. Lipizzaners are now the only breed used there, but in the early days other types, such as spotted horses, were also used. Only stallions are used in the school. Lipizzaners mature late, and they begin their training at four years old. Several years' training are needed to teach a horse the advanced movements seen in the school's displays. All the movements demonstrated in the displays are based on natural movements seen in young horses at play, and were originally developed as battle maneuvers to avoid or fend off an attacking enemy.

The Spanish Riding School's stud, founded in 1798, is now at Piber in southern Austria. Stallions standing there must have excelled in the school, and the mares

THE CAPRIOLE

The movement known as the Capriole, which is performed by the Spanish Riding School, is the ultimate expression of co-operation between horse and rider. From a standstill, the horse jumps vertically in the air to a height of about 1.8 m (6 ft), kicks out its hind feet, and lands back on the spot where it took off. In battle, this manoeuvre was used to escape when horse and rider were encircled by enemies.

Left: A Lipizzaner stallion performs the Capriole, the most difficult of the Haute Ecole movements. All the movements taught at the Spanish Riding School date from the time when horses were used in battle, and had the purpose of making the horse supple and agile so that it could evade an enemy quickly.

are also put through performance tests, to ensure that the highest standards are maintained.

Foals of gray parents are born black, and turn gray by the time they are about seven years old. At an early age they show the presence of the breed.

The Lipizzaner is intelligent and docile and, as well as being an excellent school and driving horse, it also makes a good riding horse.

The Lipizzaner is also bred in Hungary, where some are crossed with trotters to produce outstanding driving horses that have been very successful in Combined Driving competitions.

KEY FACTS

Color: Gray; born dark and lighten as they mature.
Height: 15–16 hands.
Physique: Largish head with straight profile, small ears, crested neck, compact body, powerful rounded hindquarters, strong clean legs.
Character: Intelligent, obedient, willing.
Principal uses: High-school dressage, driving.

ANCESTRY

Arab
Barb
Andalusian
Neapolitan
Kladruber
Fredericksborg

Lipizzaner

Haflinger

KEY FACTS

Color: Chestnut with flaxen mane and tail.
Height: 14 hands.
Physique: Medium-sized head with pointed muzzle, strong neck, deep girth, long broad back, well-muscled hindquarters, short legs.
Character: Hard-working, docile, frugal.
Principal uses: Mountain work, harness work, riding.

The Haflinger is the native pony of the Austrian Tyrol. Small Arab horses taken there from Italy are thought to have bred with the native mountain ponies to create the foundation stock for the breed.

The first record of the breed was made in 1868 when an Arab stallion called El Bedavi XXII was used to upgrade the local stock. All members of the breed today can be traced back to him. His son, 249 Folie, who had the typical coloring of the breed, became the foundation sire.

The Haflinger was ideal for pack and transport work in the mountains, and developed into a robust and surefooted animal. It is still used by the Austrian farmers for transporting hay. In addition, it makes a good riding and harness pony.

The Austrian state monitors the breeding of Haflingers, and its numbers are on the increase. It is still reared in the mountains, and animals are allowed to mature until the age of four before being broken in. It is also remarkably long-lived; some Haflingers are said to have worked until at least 40 years of age.

The Avelignese of northern Italy is descended from the same native stock as the Haflinger, and is popular for pack work in the mountains.

ANCESTRY

Halflinger
Native stock
Arab

Haflinger

Gelderland

The Gelderland comes from the Dutch province of Gelder, and has been developed from many different European breeds.

It was originally created from crosses of native horses with Andalusians and Norfolk Trotters to produce a versatile farm horse suitable for draft work, carriage work, and riding. During the 20th century, as the demand has declined for horses for agricultural work, the Gelderland has been crossed with the Oldenburg, Anglo-Norman, East Friesian, and Hackney to produce a lighter carriage and riding horse. Considerable work has been put into developing and fixing the type of the new breed.

With its quiet temperament, presence, good conformation, and high-stepping action, the Gelderland makes a first-class carriage-horse, and is very popular at shows in the Netherlands. It is used as foundation stock for the Dutch Warm-blood, and it has also had some success as a showjumper.

KEY FACTS

Color: Solid colors; chestnut or gray most common.
Height: 15.2–16 hands.
Physique: Plain head with convex profile, strong arched neck, deep shoulders, compact body, powerful hindquarters, high-set tail, short legs.
Character: Quiet, good-natured, active.
Principal uses: Driving, riding.

ANCESTRY

Native stock
Andalusian
Norfolk trotter
Oldenburg
Anglo-Norman
East Friesian
Hackney

Gelderland

Swedish Warm-blood

The earliest traces of horses having existed in Sweden date back to 2300 BC. However, there is not enough evidence to indicate what type of horse they were. The Swedish Warm-blood (also known as the Swedish Half-bred) was first developed some 300 years ago, to provide a good cavalry horse. Imported Oriental (ie, Barb and Arab), Andalusian, and Friesian stallions were crossed with local native mares. The breed was subsequently built up using Hanoverian, Thoroughbred, and Trakehner stallions.

In 1894 the stud book for the breed was opened. All stallions were, and still are, put through rigorous tests for conformation, character, and performance before being allowed to breed. They are also tested for their ability at showjumping, crosscountry, dressage, and harness-work.

This strict selection procedure has led to the development of one of the very best breeds of sports horse in the world today. It is a powerful, athletic horse, with good conformation and a straight, extravagant action. It excels in showjumping, eventing, and dressage. It has been so successful that only Swedish Warm-blood horses are used in the Swedish Olympic team, and it has won medals in all three competition disciplines. It is now in demand all over the world.

KEY FACTS

Color: Any solid color.
Height: 15.2–16.3 hands.
Physique: Small head with elegant features, medium-length neck, strong deep shoulders, deep body, straight back, rounded hindquarters, fine legs with short cannon bones.
Character: Intelligent, obedient, sensible, bold.
Principal uses: Riding, driving.

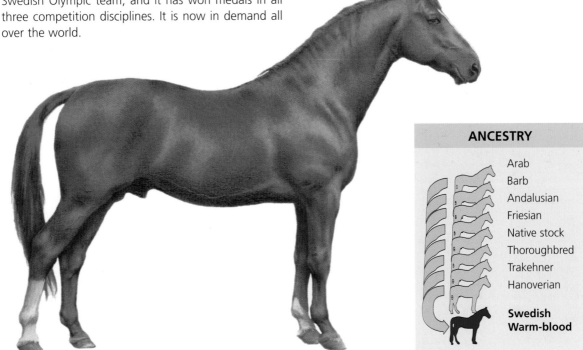

ANCESTRY

Arab
Barb
Andalusian
Friesian
Native stock
Thoroughbred
Trakehner
Hanoverian

Swedish Warm-blood

Swedish Ardennes

The Swedish Ardennes was developed during the 19th century by crossing imported Ardennes (a heavy draft breed from Belgium and northern France) with the indigenous North Swedish Horse, a light draft type with a lively temperament, descended from an ancient Scandinavian strain.

The climate and conditions of the Swedish lowlands are similar to that of the Ardennes region, and the two breeds remained similar in type. Those that were bred in the colder hill country, however, became smaller and more agile.

The Swedish Ardennes was originally developed to provide a heavy draft horse for working the land. It can withstand extreme variations in climate, it is very strong, is an exceptionally eager worker, and can survive on frugal keep. As there is now little demand for it for agricultural work its numbers are declining, although it is still used for hauling timber in mountain areas that are inaccessible to machinery.

KEY FACTS

Color: Black, brown, bay, chestnut.
Height: 15.2–16 hands.
Physique: Small head, crested neck, immensely muscular compact body, short legs, little feathering.
Character: Docile, kind, gentle, energetic.
Principal uses: Draft.

ANCESTRY

Ardennes
Swedish Horse

Swedish Ardennes

117

Fredericksborg

ANCESTRY

Andalusian
Neapolitan
Fredericksborg

KEY FACTS

Color: Chestnut most common.
Height: 15.2–16 hands.
Physique: Large plain head, strong neck, powerful shoulders, deep chest, long strong body, straight croup, strong legs.
Character: Good-tempered, active, tractable.
Principal uses: Harness, riding.

The Fredericksborg is the oldest, and was for a long time the most important, horse breed in Denmark. It was established at the Royal Fredericksborg Stud founded in 1562 by King Frederick II, and was named after him.

Andalusians and Neapolitans were used as foundation stock. The resulting breed was considered to be the best of all at the high-school equitation which was so popular in the courts of Europe from the 16th to the 18th century. In addition, it was good in harness.

The stud supplied Fredericksborgs to all the courts of Europe, and it was also popular for improving other breeds—including even the Lipizzaner. The breed was so much in demand that by the early 19th century its quality had declined, and by 1839 there were so few Fredericksborgs left there that the Fredericksborg Stud was closed. The remaining stock was used to keep the breed going, but it has had to be built up using imported blood. In 1923 Fredericksborgs began to be registered again, but even today their numbers are not great.

The purebred Fredericksborg is a very strong horse that is good in harness and for light draft work. Attempts have been made to lighten it to make it more suitable for general riding.

Knabstrup

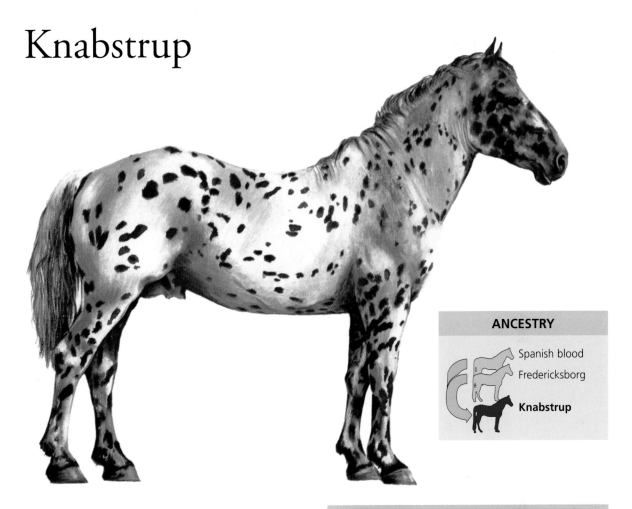

The Knabstrup is a spotted horse from Denmark that dates back to the time of the Napoleonic wars. A spotted mare of Spanish origins named Flaebehoppen was brought to Denmark and crossed with a Palomino Fredericksborg stallion. Their progeny, a spotted stallion named Flaebehingsten, became the foundation sire of the breed. As with the Appaloosa, the patterning varies from horse to horse, and no two are the same.

The Knabstrup became very popular, but unfortunately it has been bred for pattern at the expense of conformation, and as a result the type now varies considerably. At its best it is very similar to the Fredericksborg, but with a lighter build.

It is much in demand in the circus ring, but is also a good general riding horse.

KEY FACTS

Color: Spotted; Appaloosa patterns on a roan base.
Height: 15.3 hands.
Physique: Similar to but lighter than the Fredericksborg.
Character: Intelligent, tractable, active.
Principal uses: Riding, circus.

119

Døle

KEY FACTS

Color: Solid colors; usually black, brown or bay.
Height: 14.2–15.2 hands.
Physique: Varies from draft type to lighter pony type; small head, crested neck, strong shoulders, deep girth, powerful hindquarters, short legs, moderate feathering.
Character: Tough, adaptable, active.
Principal uses: Draft, riding, harness.

The Døle is an ancient breed that originates from the Gudbransdal Valley between Oslo and the North Sea coast in Norway. It is the most widespread of the Norwegian breeds, accounting for about two-thirds of the country's total equine population.

It is similar in type and appearance to the Friesian horse and the Dale and Fell ponies. This might be due to their being descended from the same prehistoric stock. However, it is more likely that crossbreeding between indigenous breeds occurred when Friesian merchants took their horses to both Norway and England between the fifth and ninth centuries. However, there are no records to verify this.

The Døle varies in size due to the fact that some have been crossed with heavy draft breeds to produce a heavy working horse, while others have been crossed with Thoroughbreds to produce a lighter type. This variety of type means that Døles can be found for heavy draft, lumber and agricultural work, general harness-work, and for riding.

An offshoot of the Døle, the Døle Trotter, was created in the 19th century by crossing the Døle with Thoroughbred blood to produce a fast, active harness horse. It is now used for racing.

ANCESTRY

Native stock
Thoroughbred
Danish draft breeds
Døle

Fjord

The Norwegian Fjord pony is an ancient and primitive breed. It is probably descended from the Asiatic Wild Horse which is depicted in prehistoric cave paintings and which it still closely resembles. Its upright mane suggests that it developed in a land where it did not have to contend with the rain.

The Fjord was the mount of the Vikings, who used it for horse-fights. The Vikings were also the first people to use a pony to pull a plow. In addition, it may have been the Fjord that they took to Iceland, and which provided the foundation stock for the Icelandic pony. Very little cross-breeding has taken place since that time, and the Fjord has probably changed little.

Selective breeding has produced a pony that is robust, hard-working, and frugal. It is also long-lived and very fertile. In addition, it has a kind, gentle nature and is very sociable. It is still indispensable in mountain areas that are inaccessible to tractors and lorries, where it is used for farm-work, pack-work, in harness, and for riding. And it has been exported to other Scandinavian countries that have no native ponies, and to Germany.

The Fjord's popularity is not just as a working pony, however. It is widespread throughout Norway as a children's pony, and for competition driving.

KEY FACTS

Color: Yellow or mouse-dun with pronounced dorsal stripe, silver and black mane and tail.
Height: 13–14.2 hands.
Physique: Concave profile, coarse upright mane, short neck merging into shoulder with no definition, powerful body, short legs, some feathering.
Character: Tireless, tractable.
Principal uses: Pack work, farm work, harness.

ANCESTRY

Asiatic Wild Horse

Fjord

Finnish

The Finnish is an amalgamation of the Finnish Universal and the Finnish Draft. These two breeds were derived from various imported breeds of draft horses that were crossed with the indigenous forest pony.

The Finnish stud book was established in 1907 and from that time the breed has been selectively bred. Finland has always developed horses on the basis of performance rather than looks or breeding, and all stallions are put through performance tests before being allowed to breed. The breed has strength, speed, stamina, agility, endurance, and is good-natured. It is easy to train, and is also lively and intelligent. There are heavier and lighter versions of the breed, and it is used as a general all-rounder, for working the land and hauling timber, for general draft work, in harness, and for riding.

The Finnish is also an excellent trotter, and many farmers enter their horses in local trotting races. In fact, a light version of the Finnish is now being bred specifically for this purpose.

KEY FACTS

Color: Chestnut, bay, brown, black.
Height: 15.2 hands.
Physique: Medium-sized head, short neck, upright shoulders, deep chest, long back, strong hindquarters, strong legs with light feathering.
Character: Quiet, docile, tractable, lively, intelligent.
Principal uses: Farm work, riding, trotting races.

ANCESTRY

Indigenous forest pony
Finnish Draft

Finnish

Icelandic

KEY FACTS

Color: Most colors.
Height: 12–13 hands.
Physique: Large head, short strong neck, deep compact body, strong clean legs, large feet, thick mane and tail.
Character: Docile, friendly, independent.
Principal uses: Draft, transport, farm work, riding.

The Icelandic pony is based on stock taken to Iceland by the Vikings when they colonized it between AD 870 and AD 930, and probably included the Fjord pony and a group of ponies from the Lotofen islands. Later, settlers from Scotland, the Orkneys, and the Shetland Islands brought their own ponies. These have blended into one breed, but various types and sizes can still be seen.

Many centuries of isolated breeding by natural selection in harsh and rugged conditions has produced ponies that are tough, agile, strong, surefooted, and full of stamina.

The Icelandic has always been invaluable to the Icelanders, and is still bred in large numbers. It is used as a pack-horse, for transport, communications, agricultural work, and riding, as well as for meat. A useful feature of the breed is that on a one-way trip it can always be relied upon to find its own way home.

A distinctive feature of the breed is that in addition to the walk, trot, and canter, they have two riding gaits: the amble and the tølt. The amble is a running walk; the tølt is a very rapid version of the amble which can increase to the speed of a canter. The tølt is particularly valuable for traveling fast across steep, icy terrain, and ponies with this gait are much in demand.

ANCESTRY

Fjord
Celtic pony
Icelandic

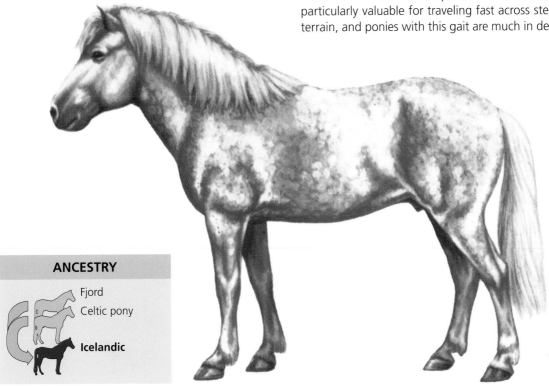

Salerno

Italy was one of the first areas in the world where horses were bred; the Etruscans are known to have bred horses there 2,500 years ago. Ever since, horse breeding has played an important part in the life of the country, and in the Salerno they produced a top-class riding horse.

The Salerno was developed during the 16th century in the Salerno area, near Naples. It evolved from cross-breeding between Andalusians and Neapolitans (a cross between Barb, Arab, and Spanish stock, and now extinct).

The Salerno was popular with the Italian army, and it is now used as a general riding horse. Although its numbers are on the decline it is playing an important part in the creation of the new Italian Saddle-horse. The Italian Saddle-Horse is being developed by crossing and upgrading the regional Italian saddle-horse breeds to produce a good general riding and competition horse.

KEY FACTS

Color: Any solid color.
Height: 16 hands.
Physique: Large refined head, good shoulders, prominent withers, strong sloping hindquarters, short legs.
Character: Intelligent, responsive.
Principal uses: Riding, cross-breeding.

ANCESTRY

Neapolitan
Andalusian

Salerno

Italian Heavy Draft

The Italian Heavy Draft was created in the 19th century in northern and central Italy. Thoroughbred, Hackney, and Arab stallions were crossed with local mares to produce a fast, active working horse. However, the strongest influence on the breed was the Breton, with which it was crossed during the early 20th century to produce a heavier, more powerful horse.

Its speed, energy, and willingness to work made it invaluable to Italian farmers before the days of mechanization. Today there is little demand for it for this type of work; its numbers are dwindling and it is kept mainly for meat.

KEY FACTS

Color: Liver chestnut with flaxen mane and tail.
Height: 15–16 hands.
Physique: Fine long head, short crested neck, powerful shoulders, deep broad chest, robust body with broad flat back, round hindquarters, muscular legs, some feathering.
Character: Lively, docile.
Principal uses: Agricultural work, meat.

ANCESTRY

Breton

Italian Heavy Draft

Andalusian

Above: This Andalusian displays all the presence and beauty for which the breed is renowned. For several centuries the Andalusian was the premier riding horse in Europe.

Right: Andalusians being driven four-in-hand. It is less commonly seen in this role than as a saddle-horse.

KEY FACTS

Color: Usually gray.
Height: 15.2–16 hands.
Physique: Broad forehead, large eyes, convex profile, long arched neck, deep short body, powerful rounded hindquarters, strong legs with short cannon bone, luxuriant mane and tail.
Character: Docile, calm, willing, proud, agile.
Principal uses: High-school, parades, bull-fighting.

The Andalusian, from the Andalusia region of southern Spain, has always been one of the most famous and sought-after breeds in Europe.

Its origins are unclear. Some people insist that it is a purebred native horse. Others believe that it developed through crosses of the native Andalusian horses; light, agile animals probably descended from the Barb, with Arabs and Barbs brought to Spain by the Moors in the 8th century.

The Andalusian type was an ideal cavalry horse due to its ability at high-school work. (The movements performed today by the Spanish Riding School of Vienna are all based on maneuvers that horses were required to perform in battle.) Demonstrations of high-school work were popular among the nobility of Europe, and from the 15th to the 18th century the Andalusian was used to found many other breeds—the Lipizzaner in Austria, the Kladruber in Bohemia (now the Czech Republic), and the Altér Real and Lusitano in Portugal. At one time it was in such demand that the exportation of breeding stock was banned on pain of death.

By the early 19th century, however, the breed's survival was in jeopardy. During the reign of Philip III of Spain, it had been crossed with several other breeds to make it heavier. During the Peninsular War (1808–14), Napoleon's marshals took the best of the stock, and many strains were wiped out. The breed's survival at this time was due to the Carthusian monks in the monasteries of Jerez, Seville, and Castello, who had been breeding Andalusians since the 15th century with great devotion and attention to purity of line. These escaped the twin ravages of cross-breeding and the Napoleonic wars. A new stud was founded and the breed began to flourish once more.

The Andalusian's influence was not confined to Europe. Many were taken to the New World by the Conquistadors, where they gradually spread throughout North and South America. In the United States the Appaloosa, the Quarter-horse, the Saddlebred, and the Mustang all have Andalusian ancestors, as do the Peruvian Paso, the Paso Fino of Puerto Rico, and the Criollo of Argentina. The Andalusian's inborn paso gait, a disjointed four-beat gait, was developed to great practical effect in the Peruvian Paso and the Paso Fino.

In Spain today, the purebred Andalusian is a great luxury. It is usually only ridden on special occasions: in street parades, in demonstrations of high-school dressage, and as the mount of the *rejoneadores* (the mounted bull-fighters).

The Andalusian has an excellent temperament. It is intelligent, docile, calm, and easy to work with. In motion it is elegant and animated. With its spectacular, high-stepping, dishing action, swinging its forelegs wide to the side as it moves, it is the center of attention whenever it appears.

ANCESTRY

Native Stock
Barb
Arab
Andalusian

Altér Real

The Altér Real is the national horse of Portugal. It was founded from the Andalusian, which it resembles quite closely.

During the 18th century, demonstrations of high-school equitation were popular among the courts of Europe, and in 1747 the Portuguese Royal Stud was founded in the Alentego Province to breed suitable horses. About 300 Andalusian mares were imported from Spain to provide foundation stock. The intelligent, athletic horses that were bred there were well suited to the demands of high school.

At the beginning of the 19th century, during the reign of Napoleon, the breed's numbers were drastically reduced. High school had by this time gone out of fashion, and for several decades Altérs were crossed with Thoroughbred, Arab, Norman, and Hanoverian blood, with the result that the breed's quality declined quite drastically.

By the early 20th century, however, the Altér's qualities were beginning to be appreciated again, and measures were taken to re-establish it by crossing pure Altérs with Andalusians.

Since 1932, the Portuguese government has supported the redevelopment of the breed through a program of selective breeding. This has resulted in a riding horse of great quality and elegance. Its intelligence, powerful physique, and high-stepping action also make it well suited to displays of high-school dressage.

KEY FACTS

Color: Bay, brown, or gray.
Height: 15–16 hands.
Physique: Medium-sized head, convex profile, strong shoulders, deep broad chest, short body, powerful hindquarters, hard legs, flexible hocks.
Character: Intelligent, temperamental, brave.
Principal use: Riding.

ANCESTRY

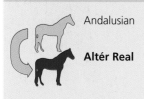

Andalusian

Altér Real

Lusitano

The Lusitano, like the Altér Real, is descended from the Andalusian, but is an altogether tougher horse. It is similar to the Andalusian, but has more Arab blood.

At one time it was used by the Portuguese cavalry; and, owing to its great strength, it was popular with farmers as a light draft and riding horse.

However, it is as the mount of the *rejoneadores* (mounted bull-fighters) of the Portuguese bullring that it is now famous. Like other horses of Andalusian descent, it has a high-stepping action and powerful hindquarters, and is easily trained in the type of high-school work that is required for bull-fighting. The fastest and most agile Lusitanos are used in the actual fight, and as it is considered a disgrace for a horse to be touched by a bull, its agility, skill, speed, obedience and great courage are tested to the full.

KEY FACTS

Color: Usually gray; can be any solid color.
Height: 15–16 hands.
Physique: Small head, straight profile, small ears, muscular neck, compact body, powerful hindquarters, long fine legs, abundant mane and tail.
Character: Intelligent, responsive, very brave.
Principal uses: Riding, bull-fighting.

ANCESTRY

Andalusian
Arab
Lusitano

Skyros

KEY FACTS

Color: Dun, brown, gray.

Height: 9.1–11 hands

Physique: Small head and ears, short neck, upright shoulders, narrow body, long legs, tendency toward cow hocks.

Character: Hard-working.

Principal uses: Pack work, farm work, children's riding pony.

In classical times, Greece was famous for its horses and horsemen. Today, however, it only has a few breeds of native pony. Of these the Skyros, from the island of Skyros, is both the best known and the smallest, the other well-known breeds being the Pindos and the Peneia.

The Skyros, an ancient pony whose origins can be traced back to the Tarpan, is finely built. On its native island it has always been used as a jack-of-all-trades, for pack work and light farm work, for transporting water, and for riding. On the mainland, it is more often used as a children's riding pony.

ANCESTRY

Tarpan

Skyros

Bosnian

The Bosnian is a native of the mountain areas of Bosnia and Herzegovina, although today it is bred in large numbers all over the Balkans. It is of ancient lineage, being descended from the wild Tarpan pony, and has been improved by crossing with Arab blood.

It shows all the characteristics of good mountain pony breeds. It is intelligent, hardy, surefooted, strong, and has great powers of endurance. The government recognizes its value for farm work and pack work, and it is selectively bred in state studs. Only stallions that have passed an endurance test, consisting of carrying a heavy load for 10 miles (16 km), are allowed to breed. It is currently being bred to increase the size.

There is still great demand for the Bosnian. In addition to being a good working pony, it is also used for riding.

KEY FACTS

Color: Dun, brown, chestnut, gray, black.
Height: 12.2–15 hands.
Physique: Compact mountain pony; thick mane and tail.
Character: Intelligent, enduring.
Principal uses: Pack work, farm work.

ANCESTRY

Tarpan
Arab

Bosnian

Tarpan

The wild Tarpan was originally a native of Poland and Russia. Some people have claimed that it was one of the original species of wild horse. However, evidence now suggests that it evolved as a cross between the original Southern Horse type of western Asia (the proto-Arab) and the Northern type of north-eastern Europe (which includes the Mongolian Wild Horse, which the Tarpan closely resembles) during the Ice Age.

Those that had been caught and domesticated were used by the peasants as general working ponies. However, Tarpan meat was considered a delicacy, and by the end of the 18th century, it had been hunted nearly to extinction. The last wild Tarpan was reported killed in 1879. The breed has since been "recreated" using domesticated Tarpan type ponies together with others that had been running free in special reserves set up at the end of the 19th century. Through a process of careful selective breeding many of the wild Tarpan's features have been restored.

Today there is a group of Tarpans roaming the state-run reserve in Popielno forest, Poland, where they are studied by scientists and archeologists.

Many breeds of pony across Europe are directly descended from the Tarpan, and still resemble it closely, including the Gotland, Norway's only native breed, the Huzul of Poland, and the Karabar from Russia.

KEY FACTS

Color: Mouse to brown with dorsal stripe, dark mane and tail, zebra stripes may appear on forelegs and inner thighs.
Height: 13 hands.
Physique: Long broad head, short thick neck, sloping shoulders, long back, thin hindquarters, fine legs.
Character: Intractable, tenacious.
Principal uses: Zoo exhibit, research; also roams wild.

ANCESTRY

Mongolian Wild Horse
Asiatic Wild Horse
Tarpan

Konik

ANCESTRY

Tarpan
Arab

Konik

The Konik is directly descended from the Tarpan. The subsequent addition of Arab blood has refined its appearance, accounting for its name, which means "little horse." It has been bred in Poland for many centuries and has influenced the development of many other Polish and Russian breeds. Today it is bred at several national stud farms as well as by local farmers.

The Konik is tough, robust, and a frugal feeder; it is also good-natured, willing, and easy to handle. It has always been popular with Polish farmers as a general working pony, and also makes a good children's riding pony.

It takes a long time to mature, but has an exceptionally long lifespan, and is very fertile.

KEY FACTS

Color: Yellow, blue, or gray dun, usually with dorsal stripe.
Height: 13.1 hands.
Physique: Large head, well-proportioned body, tendency to cow hocks.
Character: Good-natured, tough, willing.
Principal uses: Farm work, riding.

Wielkopolski

The Wielkopolski of Poland has been created by amalgamating the old Masuren and Poznan breeds.

The Masuren was a continuation of the Trakehner breed. It was bred from horses left behind at the Trakehnen stud (formerly in East Prussia) at the end of World War II. It was bred there with great care, following the principles laid down for the Trakehner breed. The Poznan was another breed based on Trakehner stock. These two breeds were extensively cross-bred, and they have now been combined into one stud book under the new breed name of Wielkopolski.

Poland has a total of 42 major stud farms, and the Wielkopolski is bred at 13 of them. All stallions must pass both conformation checks and performance tests. They also continue to work either under saddle or in harness. This careful program of selective breeding is resulting in an increase in the size and quality of the Wielkopolski.

The Wielkopolski makes a good all-rounder. It is used for light draft work on some farms, and also makes a good general riding horse. It is also proving itself as a competition horse, and this aspect of the breed is being specifically developed.

KEY FACTS

Color: Chestnut or bay most common.
Height: 16 hands.
Physique: Small head, strong neck, deep girth, medium-length back, good hindquarters, fine legs.
Character: Gentle, intelligent, active.
Principal uses: Riding, farm work.

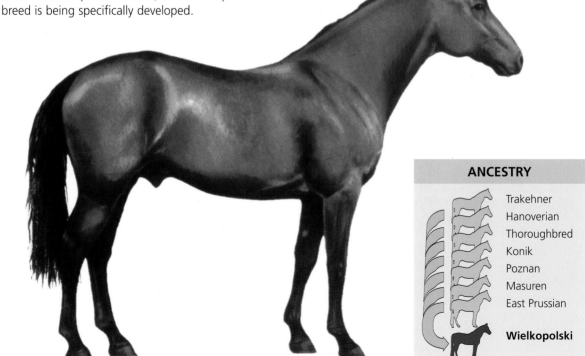

ANCESTRY

Trakehner
Hanoverian
Thoroughbred
Konik
Poznan
Masuren
East Prussian

Wielkopolski

Kladruber

The Kladruby Stud in the Czech Republic is the oldest operational stud farm in the world. It was founded by Emperor Maximilian II in 1597, and is the home of the Kladruber breed. The Kladruber is closely related to the Lipizzaner—both being directly descended from the Andalusians—but is a taller and heavier horse.

Maximilian imported Andalusians from Spain and created a new breed that had great purity of line; the only other blood being Lipizzaner from the Lipizza stud, and possibly Barb and Neapolitan. The Kladruber was bred specifically as a ceremonial coach-horse, particularly for use at the Imperial Court in Vienna.

The Kladruber's numbers had become seriously depleted by the end of World War II, and Anglo Norman, Hanoverian, and Oldenburg blood have been used to rebuild the breed. Today gray Kladrubers are still bred at the Kladruby stud, while black Kladrubers are bred at the nearby Slatinany stud.

Although the Kladruber is used for riding, it has the perfect temperament for a coach-horse, being obedient, good-natured, proud, and intelligent, and it is in this area that it excels. It is seen in marathon driving competitions; and demonstrations of Kladrubers driven 16-in-hand are popular at shows.

KEY FACTS

Color: Gray; sometimes black.
Height: 16–17 hands.
Physique: Andalusian type but larger: convex profile, strong arched neck, long body, rounded hindquarters.
Character: Proud, intelligent, obedient, good-natured.
Principal uses: Driving, riding.

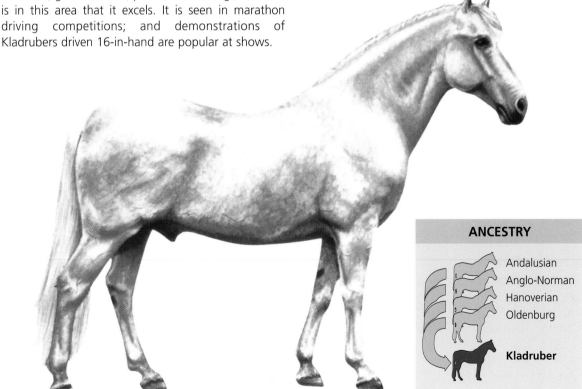

ANCESTRY

Andalusian
Anglo-Norman
Hanoverian
Oldenburg

Kladruber

Shagya Arab

ANCESTRY

Syrian Arab

Shagya Arab

The Shagya Arab was developed at the Babolna Stud in Hungary (now in the Ukraine) from about the 1830s. A group of Arab stallions and mares was imported from the desert and crossed with native Babolna stock. One of these stallions, a gray called Shagya, was a sire of great potency, and became the foundation sire of the breed. Careful selective breeding has led to the development of a specific type of Arab that is more robust than the purebred Arab.

The Shagya became known as a good cavalry and light carriage-horse, although it was also used for light draft work and general riding. It was soon in demand in central and eastern Europe, and is still bred in these countries as well as in Germany and the United States.

The Shagya makes a good general riding and competition horse. It is tough and athletic, and can thrive on poor keep.

KEY FACTS

Color: Usually gray.
Height: 15 hands.
Physique: Arab-type but a little more robust.
Character: Intelligent, good-natured, enduring.
Principal uses: Cavalry, riding, driving.

Furioso

ANCESTRY

Thoroughbred
Arab
Native stock

Furioso

Hungary has always excelled at producing high quality horses through its stud system. The Furioso is one of several Hungarian half-breds, the others being the Gidran, the Kisber, and the North Star. These horses have always excelled as harness-horses and now are highly successful in driving competitions. They have been exported all over the world.

The Furioso was established in the mid 19th century by crossing native Hungarian mares, which were small and fast, with plenty of stamina, with Thoroughbreds and Arabs. The foundation sire was an English Thoroughbred called Furioso, foaled in 1836, from which the breed takes its name.

The Furioso is an elegant and versatile horse, and is well suited for general and competition riding as well as for driving. It has been successful in the three areas of showjumping, eventing, and dressage; and in harness displays style and endurance.

The Furioso is now crossed extensively with the North Star breed (created by crossing Thoroughbreds with native mares) to produce the Mezohegyes, which is fast becoming Hungary's premier sports horse.

KEY FACTS

Color: Dark colors; often has white markings.
Height: 16 hands.
Physique: Long strong neck, powerful shoulders, long strong back, powerful hindquarters, low-set tail.
Character: Robust, intelligent, tractable.
Principal uses: Riding, driving.

137

Murakosi

Color: Chestnut with flaxen mane and tail.
Height: 16 hands.
Physique: Large head with convex profile, strong frame, pronounced dip in back, powerful hindquarters, muscular legs with light feathering.
Character: Kind, willing, active.
Principal uses: Agricultural, draft work.

The Murakosi is Hungary's draft horse, and comes from the area around the River Mura in the south of the country. It was developed during the late 19th and early 20th centuries, when there was great demand for a strong, fast draft horse.

It was created by crossing native Hungarian mares, known as Mur-Insulan, with Percherons, Ardennes, Norikers, and Hungarian Half-breds (which contained Thoroughbred and Arab blood). This produced a very strong and active draft horse that was ideal for heavy farm work. It was also used by the army.

The Murakosi was so popular that after World War I, one in every five horses in Hungary was a member of the breed. However, many were killed in World War II, and now that it is no longer much in demand for farm work, its numbers are not likely to increase again.

ANCESTRY

Native stock
Ardennes
Percheron
Noriker
Hungarian
Half-bred
Murakosi

Orlov Trotter

The Orlov Trotter is probably the best known of the Russian horse breeds. It was developed during the 18th century at a time when trotting races were very popular in Russia.

The breed was the creation of Count Alexius Grigorievich Orlov who in 1777 crossed an Arab stallion, Smetanka, with a mare of Danish origins (probably Fredericksborg). This produced a colt, Polkan, who inherited the bad as well as the good features of his father. In particular his forehand action was poor. However, when crossed with a black Dutch mare, Polkan sired a stallion, Bars 1, who was to become the foundation sire of the breed.

Further crossing with Arab, Thoroughbred, Norfolk Trotter, and Mecklenburg blood, together with in-breeding to Polkan, established the breed type, and careful selective breeding further improved it.

During the 19th century, the Orlov Trotter was the best trotting horse in the world. However, it has now been superseded by the American Standardbred. More recently, the Orlov has been crossed with the Standardbred to produce the Russian Trotter.

KEY FACTS

Color: Usually gray or black.
Height: 15.2–17 hands.
Physique: Small head, long neck, upright shoulders, broad chest, deep girth, long straight back, powerful loins, muscular hindquarters, fine hard legs with some feathering.
Character: Active, bold.
Principal uses: Trotting, harness, riding.

ANCESTRY

Danish blood
Arab
Dutch blood
Thoroughbred
Mecklenburg
Norfolk Trotter
Orlov Trotter

Don

KEY FACTS

Color: Chestnut, bay; gray most common.
Height: 15.2–16.2 hands.
Physique: Medium-sized head with wide-set eyes, long neck, long broad back, strong hindquarters, long hard legs.
Character: Calm, frugal, great stamina.
Principal uses: Riding, endurance riding.

The Don was the horse of the famous Russian Cossacks. It comes from the area around the River Don on the Russian steppes.

Originally the Don was a tough, wiry, light framed, active, Oriental type based on local stock. It more than proved its worth against Napoleon's retreating army in the winter of 1812. While the French horses died of starvation and exhaustion, the Cossacks mounted on their Dons came back to the attack again and again until they had driven the French out of Russia. And they still had the energy to make the long journey back to Moscow.

During the 19th century the breed was upgraded by crossing with Turkoman, Karabakh, and Karabir stallions that were allowed to run free with the Dons. It was further refined by crossing with Thoroughbred and Orlov Trotter blood. The Don became a larger, better-looking horse as a result.

The Don has been used to improve the Bashkersky, a versatile and enduring breed from the Bashkiria region of Russia that is used for riding and pulling sleighs. It has been used to refine the Kazakh, a highly valued riding pony due to its comfortable, ambling gait. It has been crossed with the old Kirghiz to produce a new breed, the New Kirghiz, an excellent mountain horse. And it is used as foundation stock for the Budyonny.

ANCESTRY

Turkoman
Karabakh
Karabair
Thoroughbred
Orlov Trotter

Don

Budyonny

KEY FACTS

Color: Chestnut or bay with golden sheen.
Height: 15.2–16 hands.
Physique: Small head, strong neck, long sloping shoulders, strong compact body, croup long and rounded, low-set tail, fine hard legs.
Character: Calm, intelligent, good-natured.
Principal uses: Riding, steeple-chasing.

The Budyonny is a relatively recent Russian breed, having been created in the early 20th century at the army stud at Rostov by a famous cavalry officer, Marshal Budyonny. His intention was to produce a good cavalry horse.

The breed was created by crossing Dons and Thoroughbreds—Thoroughbred stallions on Don mares achieving much better results than the other way around. Kazakh blood was also added. A highly selective breeding program was followed, with all animals being tested for speed, fitness, and endurance. As early as 1948 the breed had been fixed and was breeding to type. It was used for cavalry, harness, and draft work. It has since been used to improve other Russian regional breeds.

When the Budyonny was no longer in demand as a cavalry horse, it was re-crossed with Thoroughbred blood to produce a top-quality riding horse. It has good jumping ability, and excels in all areas of equestrian sports. It is also a successful steeplechaser due to its Thoroughbred blood.

ANCESTRY

Thoroughbred
Don
Kazakh

Budyonny

141

Akhal Teké

The Akhal Teké, from the USSR, is a pure breed of very ancient lineage. Its origins are unclear, but it is probably a strain of the Turkoman breed of Iran. There is evidence to suggest that an Akhal Teké type existed as long ago as 500 BC.

The Akhal Teké is a true desert horse. It has always been kept by the nomadic Turkmen tribes of the isolated plains of Central Asia, who took great pride in the quality and purity of their horses. They would have used it primarily as a warhorse.

The Akhal Teké has great stamina, is very fast and resilient, can survive on little food, and can tolerate extremes of temperature. It also has astonishing powers of endurance, as was proved in 1935 when a group of Akhal Tekés trekked 2,672 miles (4,300 km), from Ashkabad to Moscow, a journey which included 225 miles (360 km) of desert, which they crossed in three days without water.

The Akhal Teké has magnificent movement, and in many respects it makes a very good riding horse, but its intractable nature can make it difficult to handle.

The Akhal Teké is closely related to the Iomud, which is also directly descended from the Turkoman. At 14 hands the Iomud is smaller and more compact than the Akhal Teké, but not as fast.

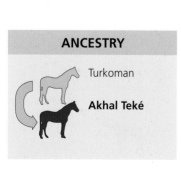

ANCESTRY

Turkoman

Akhal Teké

Tersky

KEY FACTS

Color: Gray most common; can be bay.
Height: 15 hands.
Physique: Medium-sized head with straight profile, medium-length neck and back, deep chest, muscular hindquarters, high-set tail, fine hard legs.
Character: Gentle, intelligent, enduring.
Principal uses: Flat-racing, competition, circus.

The Tersky is another recent Russian breed. It has been developed at the Tersk Stud in the northern Caucasus, originally for the purpose of producing an Arab-type racehorse.

It was founded on the Streletsk Arab, a now-extinct large Arab type based on native Ukrainian mares and Oriental stallions. The Streletsk was crossed with Arab–Dons, Thoroughbreds, and Shagyas. The progeny was reinforced with more Arab blood, until in 1948 the Tersky was recognized as a breed.

The intention was to produce a horse that had the speed and endurance of an Arab coupled with the robustness of native stock, for steeplechasing. Today, however, the Tersky is used for flat-racing. It is not as fast as the Thoroughbred, and is therefore raced against other Arabs.

It is a gentle, elegant, athletic horse with great powers of endurance. Its good movement makes it suitable for dressage. It is also used for endurance riding, and by the army; the beauty and versatility of the breed have also made it popular for the circus ring. In addition, it has been used to upgrade other Russian breeds.

ANCESTRY

Streletsk Arab

Kabardin

Don Arab

Shagya Arab

Thoroughbred

Tersky

143

Karabakh

The Karabakh is one of the former USSR's native mountain horse breeds, and comes from the Karabakh mountains in the region of Azerbaijan. It is a very ancient breed, going back to the fifth century. It contains Turkoman, Persian, and Arab blood, and has itself influenced the development of many other Russian breeds, in particular the Don. In the 18th century it became very popular and was exported to many other countries.

It is a light riding horse type, but like all mountain breeds, it is robust, surefooted, quick-witted, and calm. There are no purebred Karabakhs left, but work is being done to restore the breed.

KEY FACTS

Color: Dun, bay, or chestnut with a metallic sheen.
Height: 14.2 hands.
Physique: Small fine head, strong neck, prominent withers, strong compact body, strong hindquarters, low-set tail, fine legs and good feet.
Character: Energetic, calm, robust.
Principal uses: Riding.

ANCESTRY

Persian
Turkoman
Arab

Karabakh

Vladimir Heavy Draft

The Vladimir Heavy Draft was founded towards the end of the 19th century in the Vladimir province of Russia. However, it is now widespread throughout the former USSR.

It was developed from the Suffolk Punch and Cleveland Bay, and Ardennes and Percheron blood were also added. From about 1910 until after World War I Shire blood was also added. By 1946 the Vladimir was breeding true and the breed was considered to be fixed. From that time selective breeding using only the best stock has been practiced.

The Vladimir is a horse of great strength. It has good conformation and matures early. It is used for draft work, and also for pulling troikas.

KEY FACTS

Color: Any solid color; bay most common.
Height: 16 hands.
Physique: Small head, long strong neck, powerful shoulders, broad medium-length body, stout hindquarters, strong legs with feathering.
Character: Docile, good-tempered, active.
Principal uses: Draft.

ANCESTRY

Cleveland Bay
Suffolk Punch
Shire
Ardennes
Percheron

Vladimir Heavy Draft

Barb

The Barb is the traditional mount of the Bedouin tribes of the North African deserts. It takes it name from its native land, the Barbary Coast—now Morocco, Algeria, and Libya—where it has lived since prehistoric times.

The Barb is thought to be derived from the wild ancient horse type of northern Europe, unlike the Arab which is derived from the Asiatic type. It is distinguished from the Arab by its ram-like head and broad, straight face and muzzle, its lower-set tail, and wilder temperament.

The Barb has played an important part in founding and improving many other breeds. It was taken to Spain in large numbers by the Moors in the eighth century, and was crossed with local mares to produce the Andalusian. While the Turks occupied the eastern Mediterranean and the north coast of Africa, traders from all parts of Europe and Asia acquired Barbs and took them home to be crossed with the local horses. Charles II imported many to improve the speed and stamina of England's early racehorses, and it contributed to the founding of the Thoroughbred.

There are not many pure-bred Barbs left; crossing with the gentler Arab makes them easier to train as riding horses. The Barb has been crossed with the Arab to produce the Libyan Barb, a common breed in North Africa. It is a working horse, and is not selectively bred.

KEY FACTS

Color: Bay, brown, chestnut, black, gray.
Height: 14–15 hands.
Physique: Long refined head with straight face, crested neck, flat shoulder, long back with low-set tail, long fine legs.
Character: Quick-tempered, tough, courageous.
Principal uses: Riding, improving other breeds.

ANCESTRY

European wild stock

Barb

Caspian

The Caspian is thought to be descended from the wild native pony of Iran. This pony, which was actually a miniature horse, was used by the Mesopotamians during the third millennium BC, and it appears in carvings on the walls of Persepolis that date back to the late sixth or early fifth century BC. Since then there have been no records of the pony, and it was thought to have become extinct.

However, in 1965 a group of ponies was discovered on the southern shores of the Caspian Sea in Iran. These ponies, with their distinctive features, bear a striking resemblance to the small horses in the carvings in Persepolis. And further archeological and scientific research has confirmed that the Caspian is indeed directly descended from them. It had survived in an isolated area around the Caspian Sea, and the breed remained pure. It is now thought probable that this ancient pony is the forerunner of the Arab.

The Caspian is fast, has a free, floating action, and has great jumping ability. It is popular both as a children's riding pony, and for competition driving. Its historical importance is appreciated, and although political upheavals have disrupted its breeding in Iran, enough Caspians had been exported to the United States, Britain, and Australia to ensure its survival.

KEY FACTS

Color: Bay, brown, chestnut, gray.
Height: 10–12 hands.
Physique: Arab-type head, long neck and shoulder, narrow body with short back, tail set high, fine legs.
Character: Gentle, quick-witted.
Principal uses: Riding, driving.

ANCESTRY

Asiatic Wild Horse

Caspian

Persian Arab

KEY FACTS

Color: Gray or bay.
Height: 15 hands.
Physique: Arab-type but taller; elegant, compact body.
Character: Intelligent, lively, kind.
Principal uses: Riding, improving other breeds.

Different strains of Arab have developed which vary slightly from each other in type and size according to climate, pasture, and national preferences. The Persian Arab, raised in a temperate area, is larger and softer than its desert-bred cousins, and does not have the typical "dished" face.

The bones of a horse excavated in western Iran prove that the Arab existed there long before domestication. They also show that the Arab has changed very little since prehistoric times; man having had little influence over its build or appearance.

The Iranians have always claimed that they were the first to domesticate the Arab, and the Persian Arab is one of the oldest pure Arab lines in the world. It has been very carefully maintained through selective breeding and attention to purity of line.

Other strains of Arab in Iran have now been grouped together under the breed name of Plateau Persian. The Plateau Persian was crossed with the Thoroughbred to create a new breed, the Pahlavan.

ANCESTRY

Asiatic Wild Horse

Persian Arab

Basuto

The Basuto pony comes from Basutoland, South Africa, but is derived from the Cape Horse of the Cape Province.

Traders first imported horses, mostly Arabs and Barbs, into the Cape Province during the 17th century. Further imports of Persian Arabs and Thoroughbreds during the 18th and 19th centuries were crossed with these to produce a tough native horse, the Cape Horse, that was sold in large numbers to the British army in India as cavalry remounts. Around the 1830s, Cape Horses were used in border raids on neighboring Basutoland, and when these were over some were left behind to fend for themselves. As a result of inbreeding, harsh terrain and climate, and poor feed, the Cape Horse deteriorated into the Basuto pony. However, the harsh new conditions also made it tough, brave, and enduring. It is said to be able to carry a full-grown man up to 80 miles a day.

The Basuto was used in large numbers by the British Army during the Boer Wars. It has been used for polo and racing. It is now in demand all over South Africa as a riding pony, and particularly for trekking.

KEY FACTS

Color: Chestnut, bay, brown, gray.
Height: 14.2 hands.
Physique: Refined head, long neck, straight shoulder, long back, short legs, hard feet.
Character: Fearless, enduring.
Principal uses: General riding, trekking.

ANCESTRY

Arab
Barb
Thoroughbred
Persian Arab

Basuto

Manipur

KEY FACTS

Color: Most colors.
Height: 11–13 hands.
Physique: Long head with broad muzzle, deep chest, broad deep body, high-set tail, clean hard legs.
Character: Adaptable, lively.
Principal uses: Polo, cavalry, general working pony.

The Manipur pony has been bred in the state of Manipur, India, for many centuries. It is derived from the Mongolian Wild Horse, and has been crossed with Arab blood to improve its conformation and give it more speed.

The Manipur became famous in the 19th century as the original polo pony. Polo had been played in Asia for 2,000 years. Although the game died out in most of India, it continued to be popular in Assam and the Himalayan states. A seventh-century manuscript records polo being played in Manipur on Manipur ponies. In the 1850s, British tea-planters in Assam discovered the game being played on these fast, maneuverable ponies and took it up themselves, spreading its popularity throughout the world.

The Manipur is still used for polo in its homeland, but has been superseded elsewhere by larger, faster horses. It was also reputed to be a good cavalry horse. Being very tough, sturdy, and surefooted, and able to carry heavy loads for long distances, it has always been an invaluable working pony.

ANCESTRY

Mongolian Wild Horse

Arab

Manipur

Mongolian Wild Horse

The Mongolian Wild Horse (*Equus przewalski poliakov*) is the only surviving truly wild horse; as opposed to those that have escaped from domestication. At one time it was thought to be the basic breed from which all domesticated breeds evolved. Recent evidence suggests, however, that there were four basic groups, and that the Mongolian Wild Horse belonged to the Northern group known as the Primeval Pony.

The Mongolian Wild Horse was discovered in 1881 by Colonel Przewalski roaming the steppes of the Tachin Schara Nuru Mountains (the Mountains of the Yellow Horses), on the western edge of the Gobi Desert in Mongolia. The breed is also known as Przewalski's Horse after its discoverer. It has changed little since the Ice Age, due partly to its isolation, and partly to the ferocious temperament of the stallions. Intruders would be seen off long before they got near a herd of mares.

The Mongolian Wild Horse has always been hunted for meat, and it is now nearly extinct although measures are being taken by the Russian and Chinese governments to preserve it. Specimens are kept in zoos around the world.

It has provided the foundation stock for many domesticated breeds, including the Burma pony, the Manipur of India, and the Mongolian pony. The Mongolian pony is one of the oldest domesticated breeds in the world, and was the work pony of the nomadic tribes of Mongolia.

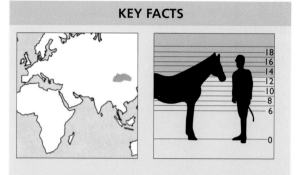

KEY FACTS

Color: Dun, usually with mealy muzzle, dorsal stripe, zebra stripes on legs.
Height: 12–14 hands.
Physique: Primitive pony type; large head, short upright mane, upright shoulders, broad short body, slight hindquarters, strong legs with short cannon bone.
Character: Timid, aggressive, great powers of endurance.

ANCESTRY

Foreign stock
Asiatic Wild Horse
Mongolian

151

Burma

The Burma pony, sometimes also known as the Shan, has been bred for a long time by the Shan hill tribes of eastern Burma.

It is closely related to the Manipur, being descended from the Mongolian Wild Horse, but has had more Arab blood added, making it larger.

It is very strong, and has always been used as a working pony. At one time it was also used by the British for playing polo, but it is too slow and unresponsive to be successful in this field.

KEY FACTS

Color: All colors.
Height: 13 hands.
Physique: Larger version of the Manipur.
Character: Active, adaptable.
Principal uses: All-round working pony.

ANCESTRY

Mongolian
Wild Horse
Arab
Burma

Java

KEY FACTS

Color: Most colors.
Height: 12.2 hands.
Physique: Slightly built, ugly.
Character: Willing, tireless.
Principal uses: Pulling two-wheel taxis, all-round work.

Indonesia's ponies are vital to the transport, communications, and agriculture of the country, and many of the islands have their own breed. The breeding of many of these ponies is supported by the state. These ponies are generally of primitive type, and over the centuries they have adapted to working in the tropical heat.

The Java is a native of the island of Java and is descended from the Mongolian Wild Horse. As well as being used for general work, it pulls the *sados*, or two-wheeled taxis, that are used on the island. It is a strong and tireless pony, and willingly pulls a full load all day.

Other island breeds include the Timor, a small, finely-built and very wise pony; the Bali, a very primitive type of pony used for pack work; the Batak from Sumatra, which has been refined and improved by crossing with Arab blood; the Gayoc, also from Sumatra; the Sumbawa, which is very similar to the Sumba; and the Sandalwood, from the islands of Sumba and Sumbawa—a fast, finely-built pony.

ANCESTRY

Tarpan
Asiatic Wild Horse
Java

153

Sumba

The Sumba is the native horse of the island of Sumba. It is a primitive type descended from a mixture of the Mongolian Wild Horse and the Tarpan.

It is used for general work on the island, but is most famous as a dancing pony. It is ridden by small boys with no saddle or bridle, and is controlled by someone on foot. It has bells tied to its knees, and dances to a tom-tom rhythm. Its performance is judged on elegance and lightness.

KEY FACTS

Color: Dun with dorsal stripe and dark points.
Height: 12.2 hands.
Physique: Primitive type, with heavy head and Stringy tail.
Character: Willing, intelligent, tough.
Principal uses: Dancing, all-round work.

ANCESTRY

Mongolian

Sumba

Australian Stock Horse

In 1971 the name Australian Stock Horse was given to Australia's oldest horse breed, the Waler.

The Waler originally developed from stock brought over from South Africa by the early settlers at the end of the 18th century. These horses were of Spanish, Arab, Barb, and Dutch origins, and could have been Cape Horses. They were crossed extensively with Thoroughbred blood from England over the next hundred years to produce a hardy, agile horse that was full of stamina. It was good for stock work on the big cattle stations, for harness work and for riding. It was also popular with the British army in India as a cavalry horse.

During the 20th century, more Thoroughbred blood has been added, along with a little Percheron and American Quarter-horse. The stud book was opened at the time that the breed's name was changed to Australian Stock Horse. Owing to the many influences on the breed, conformation varies, and it does not yet breed true to type, although progress is being made toward achieving a uniform breed type. It is a robust, Thoroughbred type of horse. It is still used for cattle-work and rodeos, and it also makes a world-class competition horse, particularly in the areas of jumping, eventing, and endurance riding.

KEY FACTS

Color: All colors.
Height: 16 hands.
Physique: Varies; Thoroughbred type with alert head, deep girth, strong back and hindquarters.
Character: Tough, willing, agile.
Principal uses: Stock-work, rodeos, general and competitive riding.

ANCESTRY

Arab

Spanish

Thoroughbred

Australian Stock Horse

Australian Pony

British native ponies have long been imported into Australia; Welsh Ponies and Shetlands being among the most popular.

The Australian Pony emerged as a result of crossing some of these breeds with Arab blood to make them lighter and more athletic. The foundation stock was created by crossing Arabs with Welsh Ponies, the most famous being a Welsh Mountain Pony stallion called Gray Light, which was imported into Australia in 1911. Subsequently Shetland, Exmoor, and Thoroughbred blood was added. By 1929 it had developed as a specific type and a stud book was opened.

The Australian Pony combines elegance and character with athleticism, and provides an excellent children's riding pony.

KEY FACTS

Color: All colors.

Height: 12–14 hands.

Physique: Arab-like head, longish neck, sloping shoulders, deep girth, short back, powerful hindquarters, tail set high, short legs, hard feet.

Character: Intelligent, lively, enduring.

Principal uses: Children's riding pony.

ANCESTRY

Arab

Welsh Pony

Exmoor

Shetland

Thoroughbred

Timor

Australian Pony

Brumby

ANCESTRY

Domesticated stock and saddle-horses

Brumby

KEY FACTS

Color: Most colors.
Height: Varies.
Physique: Varies.
Character: Intelligent; difficult to catch and train.
Principal uses: Too wild for most purposes.

The Brumby is a horse of the Australian bush that has roamed wild for over 100 years. It is descended from domesticated horses and saddle horses that were turned loose after the gold rush in the mid 19th century.

Only the cleverest and most adaptable horses survived in the harsh conditions of the Australian outback, and the Brumby developed into a tough, wily horse that is very alert. Although the quality of the horses declined due to inbreeding and poor grazing, it flourished in the wild to the point that it was considered a pest, and widespread culling has taken place. It is extremely hard to catch, and difficult to train and ride. However, "Brumby runners" herd the horses into cleverly concealed stockyards and sell the best as saddle horses.

Index

Page numbers in *italic* refer to the illustrations and captions

Aelwold, Bishop of Crediton 81
Africa 55
age, and teeth *40, 41*
aggression 21, 22, 29, *29,* 30–1
agriculture 14, *14*
Akhal Teké 142, *142*
Alaska 9
albinos *34,* 35
Alexander the Great 8
Algeria 146
allergies 46, *47*
Altér Real 79, 126, 128, *128*
amble 37
Andalusian 11, 126–7, *126–7*
Anglo-Arab 59, 96, *96*
Anglo-Norman 96, *97,* 104, 108, 115, 135
Appaloosa 62, 64–5, *64–5,* 72, 127
Arabs 11, 50, 51, 53, 56–7, *56–7,* 58–9, 96, 136, 146, 148
Ardennes 101, 103, 117, 138, 145
Argentina 75, 127
armor 16, *16*
arthritis 46
Asia 10, 12, 55, 56, 132, 142
Assam 150
Assyria 12
Australia 10, 18, 55, 60, 67, 155–7
Australian pony 156, *156*
Australian Stock Horse 155, *155*
Austria 112–14, 126
Avelignese 114
Avenches 104
Azerbaijan 144
Azoturia 47

Babolna 136
Babylonia 12
back, conformation 32
Bali 153
Balkans 131
Barb 58, 62, 75, 76, 108, 126, 135, 146, *146*
Bars 1 139
Bashkersky 140
Basuto pony 149, *149*
Batak 153
Bavarian Warm-blood 108
bay horses 34, *34,* 35
Bayeux Tapestry *16*
El Bedavi XXII 114
Bedouins 56, 146
Belgian Heavy Draft 103, *103*
Belgium 117
Bering land bridge 9
binocular vision 26
birth *44*
black horses 34, *34*
blanket clip *38*
blinkers *27*
blue eyes 35
blue roan *34*
body brushes 39
Boer Wars 149
Bohemia 126
Boomhower, Leslie 72
Bosnian 131, *131*

Boulonnais 100, 101, 111
Brabant 103
brain 24, 28
Brazil 75, 79
breeding 19, 42–5, *42–5,* 50
breeds 50–1, 54
    see also individual breeds
Breton 101, *101,* 111, 125
Britain 11, 18, 54, 58, 60, 80–93
British Army 149, 155
Brittany 101
broken wind 46
brood mares 29
brown horses 34, 35
Brumby 157, *157*
brushes 39
Bucephalus 8
Bucking *31*
Budyonny l40, 141,*141*
Budyonny, Marshal 141
Burma pony 151, 152, *152*
buses, horse-drawn *14*
buttocks, sponging 39
Byerley Turk 55

Caesar, Julius 88
Camargue 98–9, *98–9*
Campolino 79
Canada 60, 73
Canadian Cutting Horse 73, *73*
Canadian Trotter 67
canine teeth *40*
Cannon bones 32
cantering 36, *37*
Canute, King 84
Capriole 112, *112*
Carolinas 60
carriage-horses 14, 18
Carthusian monks 127
Caspian 147, *147*
Castello 127
casting coats 39
categories 50
cavalry horses 16, *17,* 19
cave paintings *11,* 12, 56, 64
Celtic pony 8, 11, 80, 82, 83, 87, 88
Central America 9
Chapman Horse 90
Charge of the Light Brigade (1854) *17*
Charles, Archduke of Austria 112
Charles II, King of England 58, 146
Cherbourg 97
chestnut horses 34, *34,* 35
Chicasaw Indians 60
chills 46
China 18, *18,* 64, 70, 151
chronic obstructive pulmonary disease (COPD) 46
circus horses 29
Cleveland Bay 90, *90,* 106, 108, 110, 111, 145
clipping *38*
Clydesdale 14
coaches, horse-drawn 14
coat 38–9
    casting 39
    color and markings 34–5, *34–5*
    grooming 39

cobs 51, 53, *53*
cold-bloods 50
colic 31, *46,* 47
collected paces 36
color, eyesight *27*
colors and markings 34–5, *34*
combined driving 18
Comet 83
commands 22–3, 28
communication 30–1
conformation 32–3, *32–3*
Connemara pony 85, *85*
Conquistadors 11, 64, 76,78, 127
Conversano 112
Cossacks 140
coughing 46
covert hacks 51
cowboys *15,* 20
cracked heels 47
cremello horses 35
Criollo 75, 75, 127
Crioulo 75, 79
cross-breeding 50
croup, conformation 33
curry combs 39
Czech Republic, the 126, 135

Dales pony 11, 82, 83, *83,* 102, 120
dandruff 38–9, *38*
dandy brushes 39
Danish Sport Horse 107
dapple gray *34*
Darius I, King *13*
Darley Arabian 59, 89
Dartmoor 81, *81*
Dash For Cash *61*
degenerative joint disease 46
Denmark 111, 118–19
Dent, Anthony 12
diarrhea 47
digestive problems 47
Dinohippus 8
diseases 46–7
dock, sponging 39
Døle 120, *120*
Døle Trotter 120
domestication 10, 12
dominant horses 31
Don 140, *140,* 141, 143, 144
donkeys 9, 35
dorsal stripes 35
Draft Breton 101
draft horses 14, *14, 15, 27,* 50
dreaming 24
dressage 18, 19, *19,* 29
driving 18
Dublin Show 19
dun horses 34, *34*
Dutch Warm-blood 115
Dynasty *107*

ears 28–9, *28–9*
East Friesian 102, 109, *109,* 115
East Prussia 105
Eastern Europe 54
Eclipse 59
eel stripes 35
Egypt 12, 64
elbows, conformation 33
Eohippus 8, *8–9*
Equus 8–9, *9,* 10

Equus przewalski poliakov 151
Etruscans 124
Europe 10, 11, 16, 54–5
eventing 19, *19*
evolution 8–9
Exmoor *8,* 11, 80, *80, 156*
extended gaits 36
eyes:
    color 35
    eyesight 26–7, *26–7*
    sponging 39, *39*

facial markings 35
Falabella 74, *74*
Far East 10, 12
farming 14, *14*
farriers 41
Favory 112
fear, smell of 31
feathering 38
feeding, foals 45
feet 40–1, *41*
    lameness 46, *47*
Fell pony 11, 82, *82,* 91, 102, 120
Fertile Crescent 12
fetlocks, feathering 38
fighting 21, *21*
Figure 63
Finnish 122, *122*
Finnish Draft 122
Finnish Universal 122
Fjord pony 85, 121,*121,* 123
Flaebehingsten 119
Flaebehoppen 119
Flanders Horse 92, 103
Flying Childers 59
foals *20,* 35, 44–5, *44–5*
fossils 8, 10
fox hunting 18, *18,* 52
France *11, 18,* 19, 59, 67, 96–101, 117
Franches Montagnes 104, *104*
Frederick II, King of Denmark 118
Fredericksborg 112, 118, *118,* 119, 139
Freiburger Saddle-horse 104
French Riding Horse 96
French Trotter 67, 97, *97,*139
Friesian 11, 82, 91, 102, *102,* 108, 116, 120
frog, hoof 41
fungal infections 47
Furioso 137, *137*

gaits 36–7, *36–7*
Galiceno 78, *78*
galloping 36, *37*
Galloway pony 58, 82, 83, 87
Garrano pony 78
Garron 87
Gayoc 153
Gelderland 115, *115*
General Stud Book 59
genetics, color 35
German Trotter 67, 139
Germany 35, 67, 103, 105–11
Gidran 137
Gobi desert 151
Godolphin Arabian 59
Gotland 132
grass sickness 47
gray horses *34*

Gray Light 156
Grayhound 67
grease, on skin 38–39, *38*
Great Horses 92, 93, 106, 110
Greece 12, *12–13*, 18, 130
Groningen 102
grooming *38*, 39

Hackney Horse 14, 37, 67, 91, *91*, 101, 115, 125
Hackney Pony 91
hacks 51, *51*
Haflinger 114, *114*
hair, coat 38
Hambletonian 10, 67
Hanoverian 19, 59, 105, 106–7, *106–7*, 108, 109, 116, 128, 135
Happy Valley, California *59*
harness horses *27*, 50, 53
harness-racing 67
Hasting, Battle of (1066) *16*
health 46–7, *46–7*
hearing 28–9, *28–9*
heavy horses 14
heels, cracked 47
heredity, color 35
Herzegovina 131
Highland pony 85, 87, *87*
hocks, conformation 32
Holstein 19, 106, 110, *110*
hooves 40–1, *41*
    cleaning *39*
hormones 42
horn, hooves 41
horse shows 18–19
horseracing 18, *18, 22*, 58–9, 67
hot-bloods 50
Hungary 113, 136–8
hunter clip *38*
hunters *50*, 51, 52
hunting 18, *18*, 52
Hussars 16
Huzul 132
Hyracotherium 8, *8–9*

Iberian horse 11
Icelandic pony 36, 37, 85, 121, 123, *123*
illnesses 46–7
impulsion 36
inadvertent learning 23
incisor teeth *40*, 41
India 18, 150, 155
Indians, North American 62, 71
Indonesia 153
influenza 46
intelligence 20–3
Iomud 142
Iran 147, 148
    see also Persia
Ireland 54, 59, 85, 94–5
Irish Draft 94, *94*, 95
Irish Half-bred 85, 95, *95*
Irish Hunter 95
Irish National Stud 28, 29
Ishoy, Cynthia *107*
Islamic Empire 16, 56–7
Italian Heavy Draft 125, *125*
Italian Saddle-horse 124
Italy 112, 114, 124–5

Janus 60

Japan 18
Java 153, *153*
jaws 40, *40*
Jennets 76, 85
Jerez 127
Joints:
    disease 46
    "locking" 25, *25*
jumping 18, 19, *19*, 20
Jura Mountains 104
Jutland 111
Kabardin 132
Karabakh 140, 144, *144*
Karabar 132
Karabir 140
Kazakh 140, 141
Kentucky 68
kicking 21, 30
Kirghiz 140
Kisber 137
Kladruber 112, 126, 135, *135*
Knabstrup 119, *119*
knights *16*
Konik 133, *133*

Lameness 46, *47*
laminitis 31, 46
laryngeal paralysis 46
Lascaux *11*, 64
learning 22–3, *22–3*
legs:
    conformation 32–3
    lameness 46, *47*
    markings 35
    movements 36–7
Libya 56, 146
Libyan Barb 146
lice 47
Limousin 96
Lipizzaner 112–13, *112–13*, 118, 126, 135
lips, sponging 39, *39*
Llanero 75
"locking" joints 25, *25*
lung diseases 46
lunge reins 22
Lusitano 126, 129, *129*
lying down 24–5, *25*

Maestoso 112
manes 38, 39
Mangalarga 79, *79*
Manipur 150, *150*, 151, 152
mares:
    breeding 29, 31, 42, *42*
    with foals 44–5
    giving birth *44*
    stud books 50
markings 34–5, *35*
Marsh Horse 110
martingales 26
Massachusetts 63
Masuren 134
mating 31, 42, *43*
Maximilian II, Emperor 135
Mecklenburg 107, 139
Merlin 89
Mesopotamia 147
Messenger 66–7
Mexico 64, 78
Mezohegyes 137
Middle East 10, 55, 56
Minhos 78

Mohammed, Prophet 56
molars 40, *40*
molting 39
Mongolia 18
Mongolian pony *11*, 151
Mongolian Wild Horse *9, 11*, 132, 150, 151, *151*, 152, 153, 154
Mongols 18
Moors 11, 57, 98, 100, 126, 146
Morgan 63, 63, 67, 68, 69, 102
Morgan, Justin 63
Morocco 146
movement 36–7, *36–7*
mud fever 47
Mur-Insulan 138
Murakosi 138, *138*
music 28–9
Mustang 60, 62, *62*, 127

Napoleon I, Emperor 127, 140
Narragansett Pacer 67 , 68, 69
navicular disease 46
Neapolitan 110, 112, 118, 124, 135
Neapolitano 112
neck, conformation 33
neighing 31
Netherlands 102, 115
nettle rash 47
New Forest pony 84, *84*
New Zealand 67
Nez Perce Indians 64
nomads 10
Norfolk Trotter 91, 93, 97, 101, 102, 115, 139
Noriker 138
Norman 104, 108, 128
Norman Conquest *16*
Normandy 96, 97
North Africa 146
North America 8, 9, 10, 11, 54, 60–73, 127
North Star 127
North Swedish Horse 117
Norway 120–1, 132
nostrils, sponging 39, *39*

Old English Black 92
Old Welsh Cart-horse 89
Oldenburg 102, 108, *108*, 109, 115, 135
Olympic Games 19
"on Ihe bit" 36
origins of the horse 8–11
Orlov, Count Alexius Grigorievich 139
Orlov Trotter 67, 102, 139, *139*, 140

pacing 36, 37, 67, *67*
pack horses 14
Pahlavan 148
paints 35
Palm Beach *67*
Palomino *34*, 35, 62, 70, 71
parasites *38*, 47
park hacks 51
Parthenon Frieze *12*
Paso breeds 37, 76
Paso Fino 77, *77*, 127
pasterns, conformation 33
pedigrees 50

Peneia 130
Peninsular War 127
Percheron *15*, 100, *100*, 101, 138, 145,155
Persepolis 147
Persia 12, *13*, 16, 18, 64
Persian Arab 148, *148*, 149
"personal space" 30
Peru 76
Peruvian Stepping Horse 76, *76*, 77, 127
Philip III, King of Spain 127
Piber 112
piebalds *34*, 35
Pindos 130
pink skin 34–5
pinna 28
Pinto 35, 62, 71,*71*
Plateau Persian 148
Pluto 112
points of the horse 32–3, *32–3*
Poland 105, 132–4
police horses *15*
Polkan 139
polo 18, *18*, 150
ponies 50, 52–3, *52*
Pony of the Americas *52*, 72, *72*
Portuga l78, 126, 128–9, 132
Postier Breton 101
Postier Percheron 100
Poznan 134
pregnancy 42–3
problem-solving 20
Przewalski, Colonel 151
Przewalski's Horse 151
Puerto Rico 77, 127
punishments 23

Quarter-horse *15*, 60, *60–1*, 62, 73, 127, 155

racehorses 18, *18, 22*, 58–9, 67
rack 36, 37
rash, nettle 47
reasoning power 20
relationships with humans 30, 31
respiratory problems 46
retina 26
rewards 23
Rhineland 103
riding ponies 52–3, *52*
ringworm 47
roan *34*
roaring 46
rodeo horses *31*
rolling *38, 46*
Romans 11, 12, 82, 88, 90, 98, 102
Rotteler draft breed 108
Roussin 101
Royal Canadian Mounted Police *15*
Russia 9, 12, 67, 132, 139–45, 151
Russian Trotter 139
Ryan's Son *95*

Sable Island Pony 73
Saddle-horse, American 36
saddle sores *46*
Saddlebred 51, 63, 68, *68*, 69, 127
Salerno 124, *124*

Sandalwood 153
Scandinavia 55
Schleswig Heavy Draft 110, *111*
Schleswig-Holstein 110–11
Schwieken horse 105
Scotland 86–7, 123
Scots Grays *17*
Selle Francaise 96
Seville 127
sexual organs *42–3*
Shagya Arab 104, 136, 136, *143*
Shaun 152
sheath, sponging 39
Shetland pony 72, 74, 85, 86, *86,* 156
Shire 14, *14, 27,* 92, *92*
shoes 41
shoulders, conformation 33
showjumping 18, 19, *19*
shows 18–19, 51, 52, 53
sight 26–7, *26–7*
Siglavy 112
sinus infections 46
skewbalds *34,* 35
skin 38–9
skin diseases 47
skull *40*
Skyros 130, *130*
sleep 24–5, *24–5*
slow gait 37
smell, sense of 30, 31
Smetanka 139
sobreandando 37
Sorraia 132
sounds, hearing 28
South Africa 60, 67, 149, 155
South America 9, 54, 60, 74–9, 127

Southern Europe 55
Spain 11, *16,* 57, 62, 64, 70, 75, 76, 78, 126–7, 146
Spanish Armada 85
Spanish Riding School *23,* 112–13, *112,* 126
sperm 42
sponges 39, *39*
sports 18–19, *18–19*
squealing 31
stable rubbers 39
stables 24–5
stag hunting 18
stallions 29, 31 ,42, *42,* 50
Standardbred 63, 66–7, *66–7,* 69, 97, 139
startle response 20, 21, *21*
stepping pace 37
Stone Age 37
strangles 46
strawberry roan *34*
Streletsk Arab 143
stud books 50
Suffolk, Lady 67
Suffolk Punch 93, *93,* 111, 145
Sumatra 153
Sumba 153, 154, *154*
Sumbawa 153
Sweden 116–17
Swedish Ardennes 117, *117*
Swedish Half-bred 59, 116, *116*
Swedish Warm-blood 59, 116
sweet itch 47
Swiss Half-bred 110
Switzerland 104

tails 30, 38, 39

Tarpan 9, 11, 130, 131,132, *132,* 133, 154
tartar, on teeth 40
Tartars *18*
teaching horses 22–3, *22–3*
teeth 40, *40–1*
tendon injuries 46
Tennessee Walking Horse 63, 69, *69*
Tersky 143, *143*
Texas *15*
thinking ability 20–1
Thoroughbreds *18,* 19,50,51. 52, 53, 58–9, *58–9*
threats, reacting to 21, *21*
three-day events 19
Timor 153
tølt 36, 37
trace clip *38*
training 22–3, *22–3*
Trakehner 19, 105, *105,* 106, 107, 108, 116,134
transport, horse-drawn 14, *14*
Trotters 14
trotting 36, *36*
Turkoman 140, 142, 144
Turks 58, 59
tushes *40*
Tyrol 114

udder, sponging 39
Ukraine 136
United States of America 18, 59, 60–72, 127

Venezuela 75
vets 40, 46
Victoria, Queen 84

Vienna 112
Vikings 111, 121, 123
Virginia 60
vision 26–7, *26–7*
Vladimir Heavy Draft 145, *145*
vocal calls 31

Waler 155
walking 36, *36*
wall eyes 35
war horses 14, 16, *16–17*
warbles 47
warm-bloods 50–1
water brushes 39
weaning foals 45
Welsh Cob 53, 63, 89
Welsh Mountain Pony 88, 156
Welsh Ponies 88–9, *88,* 156
Western Europe 54
Westphalian 107
whinnying 31
whips 23, 27
white horses 34–5
Wielkopolski 105, 134, *134*
wild horse 121, 132, 151. *151*
wind galls 46
withers, conformation 33
working horses 14, *14–15*
World War I 16, *17*
worm infestation 47
Wurttemburg 105

Yorkshire Coach Horse 90
Yorkshire Trotter 91
Yugoslavia 112, 131

zebra marks 35
zebras 9, *9*

Credits

Images on the following pages are the copyright of Bob Langrish: 2, 6, 14B, 15T, 15B, 18T, 18M, 18B, 19T, 19M, 19B, 20BL, 20BR, 22T, 22B, 23, 30T, 31B, 37T, 39L, 39R, 43, 44T, 44B, 45T, 45C, 45B, 46B, 47T, 47B, 49, 50, 51, 52, 53, 56, 57, 59, 61, 65B, 67, 74, 95, 107, 112.

Other images in this book are the copyright of:
Anne Bazalik
Bridgeman Art Library
Mary Evans Picture Library
Kit Houghton
Peter Newark's Military Pictures
Sally-Anne Thompson/Animal Photography

Although we have made every effort to trace and acknowledge all copyright holders, Quarto would like to apologize if there should be any omissions.